# INSTRUMENT OF YOUR PEACE

The art of Catholic pastoral care

Margaret Ghosn

Published by Acorn Press
An imprint of Bible Society Australia
ACN 148 058 306 | Charity licence 19 000 528
GPO Box 4161
Sydney NSW 2001
Australia
www.acornpress.net.au | www.biblesociety.org.au

© Margaret Ghosn, 2024. All rights reserved.

ISBN 978-0-647-53357-4

First published by Morning Star Publishing in 2016, ISBN 978-1-925-20824-5

Margaret Ghosn asserts her right under section 193 of the *Copyright Act 1968* (Cth) to be identified as the author of this work.

Scripture quotations are from the *New Revised Standard Version Bible,* copyright © 1989 the Division of Christian Education of the National Council of Churches of Christ in the United States of America.
Used by permission. All rights reserved.

Apart from any fair dealing for the purposes of private study, research, criticism or review, no part of this work may be reproduced by electronic or other means without the permission of the publisher.

 A catalogue record for this book is available from the National Library of Australia

Cover and text design and layout by John Healy

# Table of Contents

*Introduction* ................................................................ 1

*Chapter 1: Scriptural basis for pastoral care* ............. 3
    The God of the Old Testament ........................... 3
    The story of Jesus ................................................. 5
    New Testament writings ..................................... 10

*Chapter 2: The meaning of suffering* ....................... 12
    Why do we suffer? ............................................... 13
    Scripture and suffering ....................................... 14
    Suffering, the Cross and Redemption ............... 16
    Reasons for suffering .......................................... 18

*Chapter 3: Pastoral care as a response to human needs* ... 23
    Tracing the historical development of the ministry of pastoral care ... 24
    Defining pastoral care for today ......................... 26
    Generic chaplaincy - just spiritual care? ........... 29
    Christian pastoral care ........................................ 31

*Chapter 4: Pastoral care qualities* ............................ 34
    What to avoid in pastoral care ........................... 34
    What is recommended in pastoral care ............ 35
    Faith ...................................................................... 36
    Hope ..................................................................... 37
    Love ...................................................................... 39
    Presence ............................................................... 40
    Compassion ......................................................... 41
    Prayer ................................................................... 42
    Conclusion ........................................................... 44

*Chapter 5: Pastoral care to the young* ..................... 45
    Generations Y and Z ........................................... 45
    Young people today ............................................ 46
    Pastoral care of the young ................................. 47

*Chapter 6: Pastoral care to the sick* ......................... 49
    Religion as beneficial - Studies .......................... 49
    Catholic Health Care in Australia ..................... 51
    Hospital chaplaincy ............................................ 52
    Practical care ....................................................... 55

*Chapter 7: Pastoral care of the elderly* 62
    Australian Bureau of Statistics 63
    Age categories 64
    The dignity of the elderly 66
    Practical care 67
    Aged care facilities 72

*Chapter 8: Pastoral care of the dying* 76
    Belief in life after death 76
    Stages of death 78
    Palliative and hospice care 80
    Practical care 82
    The ethical issue of life support 85

*Chapter 9: Pastoral care to the grieving* 89
    Stages of grief 89
    Christian meaning after death 92
    Funerals 94
    Practical care 95

*Chapter 10: Sacramental dimension* 100
    Our sacramental role 100
    The sacrament of baptism 101
    Sacrament of the Eucharist 102
    Sacrament of reconciliation 103
    Sacrament of anointing of the sick 104
    Final thought 104

*Chapter 11: The stations of the Cross –Accompanying the sick and dying* 106

*Bibliography* 110

# *Introduction*

Let us begin our understanding of pastoral care with that well known ode attributed to Saint Francis of Assisi.

> Lord, make me an instrument of your peace;
> where there is hatred, let me sow love;
> where there is injury, pardon;
> where there is doubt, faith;
> where there is despair, hope;
> where there is darkness, light;
> and where there is sadness, joy.
> O Divine Master, grant that I may not so much seek
> to be consoled as to console;
> to be understood, as to understand;
> to be loved, as to love;
> for it is in giving that we receive,
> it is in pardoning that we are pardoned,
> and it is in dying that we are born to Eternal Life. Amen.

The call to be an instrument of God's love and peace is at the heart of Christian faith and the basis of pastoral care. Yet how honest, willing or capable are we of approaching others with quality care? At the back of our mind lingers the possibility of rejection, of failure, of not knowing what to do. Such fears are the common lot of humankind.

In the Old Testament we read of Jonah's reluctance to care for the people of Nineveh. Then the LORD said, 'You are concerned about the bush, for which you did not labour and which you did not grow; it came into being in a night and perished in a night. And should I not be concerned about Nineveh, that great city, in which there are more than a hundred and twenty thousand people who do not know their right hand from their left, and also many animals?' (Jonah 4:9-11). This passage reveals the darker side of humanity where we seek mercy for ourselves but justice for others.

We also read in Luke 5:8 where Simon Peter reacts with fear in the face of unexpected love. Falling down at Jesus' feet, he cries out, 'Go away from me, Lord, for I am a sinful man!' In reading Exodus we discover Moses and his muttering excuses, which convey the dread in many of us, 'But suppose they do not believe me or listen to me.' Again we hear of Moses' fear, 'O my Lord, I have never been eloquent, neither in the past nor even now that you have spoken to your servant; but I am slow of speech and slow of tongue.' And a third time Moses pleads, 'O my Lord, please send someone else' (Ex 4:1, 10, 13). Like Moses, we are not always sure or confident of what we are capable of. Yet despite one's hesitancy, with time, experience, and coming to know God, one can become a great leader as Peter and Moses proved. This is because pastoral care emerges from our own acquaintance with suffering and grief.

This book has been designed to provide you with an in-depth understanding of what we mean by offering pastoral care to the young, elderly, sick, dying and grieving.

# Chapter 1: Scriptural basis for pastoral care

## The God of the Old Testament

The Bible is a collection of stories written and re-written over many centuries that convey a religious message. It is the story of the journey into faith of a people of God. Along the way experiences are gained, insights deepened and ways of understanding translated into new modes of being and living. The growing perception of the one God characterised by tender love and forgiving compassion, is enacted out in love of neighbour. So let us take a closer look at Scared Scripture.

From the commencement of Genesis (the first book of the Bible) there is the understanding that God creates all things, including humans, with loving kindness. God is fond of life, as we read, 'God saw everything that he had made, and indeed, it was very good' (NRSV Gen 1:31). Life, including human life, is blessed from the moment of creation, and is held dearly. All life is gift and finds its fulfilment in God.

Now as creations of God, humans are not perfect, and as the story unravels humans find themselves in strife. Yet despite the suffering caused by wrong decisions and toil that must be endured, God never forsakes man and woman, as we read in Gen 3:21, 'and the Lord God made garments of skins for the man and his wife, and clothed them.'

The ancestral stories are told in the book of Genesis with the importance of relationship not only with God but with one another emphasized. When Abraham dies, 'His sons Isaac and Ishmael buried him' (Gen 25:9). What was conceived as a rift between brothers is reconciled in the presence of a beloved but dying parent. Again when Isaac died, 'his sons Esau and Jacob buried him' (Gen 35:29). At Jacob's death, Joseph went with all his servants and household (Gen 50:7-8) to bury his father. For it is in death and grief that barriers are overcome and reconciliation can take place.

In the Book of Exodus we read of God who hears the cry of the afflicted and responds with mercy and saving help towards the Israelites, through Moses. We read in Ex 3:7, 'Then the LORD said, 'I have observed the misery of my people who are in Egypt; I have heard their cry on account of their taskmasters. Indeed, I know their sufferings.'
Through Moses, God is determined to save the Israelites from further oppression and suffering. God continues that promise of compassion and mercy as we read in the Prophetic Books.

The Prophets articulate the compassion and mercy of a God who desires above all else a loving and faithful relationship with people, as was expressed in the covenant. Listed below are a number of passages that convey a deep understanding of God's care.

> **Is 41:10, 13** - Do not fear, for I am with you, do not be afraid, for I am your God; I will strengthen you, I will help you, I will uphold you with my victorious right hand. . . For I, the LORD your God, hold your right hand; it is I who say to you, 'Do not fear, I will help you.'
>
> **Is 46:4** - Even to your old age I am he, even when you turn grey I will carry you. I have made, and I will bear; I will carry and will save.
>
> **Is 49:13** - For the LORD has comforted his people, and will have compassion on his suffering ones.
>
> **Is 49:15-16** - Can a woman forget her nursing-child, or show no compassion for the child of her womb? Even these may forget, yet I will not forget you. See, I have inscribed you on the palms of my hands.
>
> **Jer 29:11-14** - For surely I know the plans I have for you, says the LORD, plans for your welfare and not for harm, to give you a future with hope. Then when you call upon me and come and pray to me, I will hear you. When you search for me, you will find me; if you seek me with all your heart, I will let you find me, says the LORD. . .
>
> **Hos 11:3-4** - Yet it was I who taught Ephraim to walk, I took them up in my arms; but they did not know that I healed them. I led them with

cords of human kindness, with bands of love. I was to them like those who lift infants to their cheeks. I bent down to them and fed them.

**Micah 6:8** - He has told you, O mortal, what is good; and what does the LORD require of you but to do justice, and to love kindness, and to walk humbly with your God.

The Scriptures reveal a patient God who bears with human imperfections as they struggle in the journey of faith. It is an encouraging God, who picks up, comforts and sends one back into the fray with greater enthusiasm.

In the encounter with the collection of Writings in the Old Testament, there is emphasis on right relationships and advice for best living. Below are a number of passages from the Writings as food for thought.

**Sirach 7:34** Fail not to be with them that weep, and mourn with them that mourn. Be not slow to visit the sick: for that shall make you to be beloved.

**Psalm 8:3-4** When I look at your heavens, the work of your fingers, the moon and the stars that you have established; what are human beings that you are mindful of them, mortals that you care for them?

**Pm 30:2** I cried to you for help, O Lord my God, and you healed me.

**Pm 147:3** He heals the broken-hearted, and binds up their wounds.

From the journey of the Israelites into faith, we leave the Old Testament and enter into the journey with Jesus.

## The story of Jesus

The journey as told throughout the Bible, leads us to the New Testament, where we encounter Jesus who 'came that they may have life, and have it abundantly' (Jn 10:10). What immediately strikes one on encountering

Jesus in the Scriptures, is a person of great depth and profound wisdom, combined with generosity of heart, sensitivity toward the needy, compassion for those in despair, and possessing infinite love for neighbour.

Jesus is a man who heals heart, mind and body. He seeks and finds, he listens and responds, touches and forgives, and he embraces and builds up. People approach because there is nothing to fear, 'He will not break a bruised reed nor quench a smouldering wick' (Mt 12:20). People are drawn to him because he speaks a truth that resonates in hearts and minds. He is a presence that brings others to fullness of life.

In Jesus, the Word of God took flesh among us as 'one like us in all things except sin' (Heb 4:15). Jesus reaffirms the dignity of every human as a person created in the image of God and invites all to a communion of life with God. Jesus is one who comes to offer pastoral care.

The term pastoral care is associated with the shepherding imagery of ministry. It has its origins in 'to pastor', which implies looking after the safety of one's livestock. The shepherd imagery is seen throughout the Scriptures including Ps 23, Is 40:11, Jer 31:10, Ezek 34:1-24, Acts 20:28, 1 Pet 5:2-4 and Rev 7:17. In John 10, what is emphasised is the shepherd's self giving and steadfast love, his fidelity, courage and willingness to know each sheep. Yet while rich in symbolism, the idea of a shepherd caring for the sheep can foster a sense of paternalism. It needs to be balanced by the idea of pastoral care as empowering individuals and communities to greater responsibility for the direction of their lives, as we witness in Jesus' care for others.

Jesus emphasized the call to love, 'I give you a new commandment, that you love one another. Just as I have loved you, you also should love one another. By this everyone will know that you are my disciples, if you have love for one another' (Jn 13:34-35). His example has inspired men and women over the ages to reach out to people who are sick or impaired, to those who mourn the death of a loved one, and to those forced to the margins of society. In caring for those in need we meet Jesus himself (Mt

25:31-46) and participate more deeply in the mystery of his death and resurrection, through grace that transforms human life. So let us take a closer look at a number of features of Jesus, including his ability to care, heal, guide, sustain, reconcile and affirm.

Jesus showed care. 'And when he saw the crowds he felt sorry for them because they were harassed and dejected like sheep without a shepherd' (Mt 9:36). The Greek word used conveys a gut wrenching empathy and anger that 'things should not be like this.' Jesus was deeply moved by the daily sufferings of the poor and more so that they had been let down by their religious elders. It is evident (particularly in Mark's Gospel), that Jesus is a person who listens to and responds from his emotions (compassion, frustration, anger, sadness etc). He was motivated by a concern that people be made whole again.

Jesus performed miracles and healings to free people from suffering and to reassure them that God is at work in their lives. He also showed that the faith of other people can be the vehicle of God's healing, a sign of God's forgiveness and love. Jesus often healed and restored personal integrity before concern for sin. He offered reassuring and affirming presence. Jesus also appointed seventy others and sent them on their way to cure the sick and preach the Kingdom of God (Lk 10:1, 8).

At times we see Jesus as prophetic and challenging (Mk 10: 17-22, Jn 13: 21-30). By being himself, by his preaching and teaching, the Reign of God was made present. Jesus invites others to witness to the good news, to be salt of the earth and a light to the world (Mt 5:13-16).

Jesus' care sustains and nourishes persons and relationships. Humans need to be heard and understood when feeling anger, pain or fear. Pastoral care is not just about serving one in need, but about doing it with love, 'When Jesus saw her weeping, and the Jews who came with her also weeping, he was greatly disturbed in spirit and deeply moved... Jesus began to weep' (Jn 11:33, 35). The ability to empathise was a valued quality of Jesus.

Jesus was concerned with the reconciliation of relationships that were fractured. These relationships include with God, oneself, others, society and the created world. As Scripture reads, Jesus 'unrolled the scroll and found the place where it was written, "The spirit of the Lord is upon me, because he has anointed me to bring good news to the poor. He has sent me to proclaim release to the captives and recovery of sight to the blind, to let the oppressed go free, to proclaim the year of the Lord's favour"' (Lk 4:17-18; cf. Is 61:1-2).

Affirmation is necessary for human growth. Each person longs to be appreciated and praised. 'Well done good and faithful servant' is a frequent image used in the Gospels by Jesus. Helping people to develop and reach their potential manifests God's presence. As Anthony Gittins writes:

> Jesus the stranger was also a catalyst: he accelerated the pace of change, caused unimaginable reactions, offered unexpected alternatives, enabled healing to happen, precipitated novelty. People came to expect something exciting when he was around, and he in turn was excited by their faith-filled responses. Yet, no one could predict his actions any more than he could control their response to grace. Nevertheless, in this community, the reign of God was promoted. Together, they ministered: the woman at the well and the one who bathed his feet with her hair; the Gerasene demoniac and the little man in the tree whose table and soul were graced by Jesus. Jesus could only minister where there was trust. The same could be said of his disciples, then and now.[1]

Jesus also revealed God's love and compassion through stories he told. Such an example is the parable of the Good Samaritan (Lk 10:29-37), where a beaten man lies dying on a main road. 'By chance' (v31) some people pass along. One is invited here to see all experiences as opportunities for growth and encounter with Christ. However as we read, the Priest and Levite saw 'trouble' instead of need. It is only the Samaritan

---

[1] Anthony J. Gittins, *Reading the Clouds. Mission Spirituality for New Times*, (Strathfield: St Pauls, 1999), 88.

who saw a 'chance' at helping the dying man. We are meant to be more than 'passersby' as the parable suggests.

The Good Samaritan stops and offers pastoral care. It is about noting the situation around you, stopping and taking time out for the person in need. In First Aid the rule is DR ABCD, standing for Danger, Response, Airway, Breathing, Compressions and Defibrillation. The Good Samaritan notes not only the danger he might be in, but also the risk to the victim's life. He then checks the response of the dying man. Yet more than just offering First Aid, the Good Samaritan 'was moved with pity' (v33). This pity is also seen in the lost son's father (Lk 15:20) and in the widow of Naim (Lk 7:13).

The Samaritan's mercy, risk, generosity and practical attention to the needs of the afflicted, indicate God's concern for those people whom others despise or condemn. God comes to bind up the wounds of the suffering, through unexpected love. Mercy sees the need and responds with compassion, just as God does.[2] God's mercy breaks through all human restrictions of how one should act towards sinners.

The parable in Luke intends to show that becoming a neighbour means showing mercy, by identifying with those in need, even beyond the bounds of ethnic or religious groups. The imperatives 'go and do' (v 37), imply that Jesus commands the lawyer to go and do this by lifelong conduct. It is not who is my neighbour, but how can I be a neighbour (v36). The parable is a challenge and reminder we are responsible for one another.

The call to be merciful is also clearly witnessed in the parable of Judgment Day in Mt 25:34-40. If we are to be more like Jesus, we must imitate him in his humanity. As Christians who belong to the Body of Christ (1 Cor 12: 24, 26-27), we are called to embody the same

---

[2] Alan R. Culpepper, *The New Interpreters Bible: Luke* Vol IX, (Nashville: Abingdon, 1995), 230.

compassion and hope. We are to feed, clothe, welcome, nurture and visit the marginalised members of our society.

It is in our human nature to feel compassion for those who cry in desperate need. In fact Christians are generous givers, opening their purses to numerous appeals including Caritas, the Salvos and St Vincent de Paul. In instances of floods or bushfires their hearts and prayers go out to those crying for help. This capacity to empathise with others is our call to the best of the human condition. Anthony J Gittins puts it:

> Jesus the prophet will disclose forgotten or unknown aspects of God. He will speak of God's compassion for every single person, and God's utter lack of vindictiveness or partiality. He will preach good news of community and inclusion and hope to a people steeped in a world of hierarchy and exclusion and fatalistic despair. This will bring upon him the opprobrium and self-righteousness of the privileged classes. It will also have such liberating potential for despised and condemned people as to give them a new lease on life, turning at least some of them into a community of radical itinerants or healed healers.[3]

## New Testament writings

Alongside the Gospels, the New Testament is rich in letters of counsel. Among them are words of wisdom by Saints Paul and John. They convey the abundant love of Jesus, whose death offers redeeming hope.

> **Rom 12:5-15** So we, who are many, are one body in Christ, and individually we are members one of another. We have gifts that differ according to the grace given to us: prophecy, in proportion to faith; ministry, in ministering; the teacher, in teaching; the exhorter, in exhortation; the giver, in generosity; the leader, in diligence; the compassionate, in cheerfulness. Let love be genuine; hate what is evil, hold fast to what is good; love one another with mutual affection; outdo one another in showing honour. Do not lag in zeal, be ardent in spirit, serve the Lord. Rejoice in hope, be patient in suffering, persevere in

---

[3] Gittins, *Reading the Clouds. Mission Spirituality for New Times*, 111.

prayer. Contribute to the needs of the saints; extend hospitality to strangers. Bless those who persecute you; bless and do not curse them. Rejoice with those who rejoice, weep with those who weep.

**2 Cor 11:29** Who is weak, and I am not weak? Who is made to stumble, and I am not indignant?

**Eph 4:32** Be kind to one another, tender-hearted, forgiving one another, as God in Christ has forgiven you.

**Hb 13:3** Remember those who are in prison, as though you were in prison with them; those who are being tortured, as though you yourselves were being tortured.

**1 Jn 4:7, 9** Beloved, let us love one another, because love is from God; everyone who loves is born of God and knows God. . . God's love was revealed among us in this way: God sent his only Son into the world so that we might live through him.

Christians are invited into discipleship and the healing ministry of Christ. Baptised, they are sent out into the world to offer the loving compassion of Christ to all. Put simply they are called to offer pastoral care.

Christian understanding of God is at the heart of ministry and determines the way care is offered to others. Aside from the Bible which is the primary source of inspiration, there are also many writings, Church documents and encyclicals that urge one to minister as Jesus did. In Vatican II's *Gaudium et Spes*, the opening words remind Christians they can meet God in every human encounter, 'The joys and the hopes, the griefs and the anxieties of the men of this age, especially those who are poor or in any way afflicted, these are the joys and hopes, the griefs and anxieties of the followers of Christ. Indeed, nothing genuinely human fails to raise an echo in their hearts.' With the knowledge that God loves us and that we too are called to share this love, let us see how we are to respond to the joys and griefs of our human condition.

# *Chapter 2: The meaning of suffering*

Struggle changes us; it grows us up. It takes the dew off the rose and the gilt off the silver. It turns the fantasies of life into reality. But struggle does more than that. It also gives life depth and vision, insight and understanding, compassion and character . . . once we have struggled with something that stretches the elastic of the spirit, we are worthy to walk with others in struggle, too. Then we're ready to listen. Then we're able to lead – **Joan Chittister**[4]

One day, as we came returned from work, we saw three gallows, three black ravens, erected on the *Appelplatz*. Roll call. The SS surrounding us; machine guns aimed at us: the usual ritual. Three prisoners in chains – and, among them, the little *pipel*, the sad-eyed angel.

The SS seemed more preoccupied, more worried, than usual. To hang a child in front of thousands of onlookers was not a small matter. The head of the camp read the verdict. All eyes were on the child. He was pale, almost calm, but he was biting his lips as he stood in the shadow of the gallows.

This time, the *Lagerkapo* refused to act as executioner. Three SS took his place.

The three condemned prisoners together stepped onto the chairs. In unison, the nooses were placed around their necks.
 'Long live liberty!' shouted the two men.
But the boy was silent.
 'Where is merciful God, where is He?' someone behind me was asking.

At the signal, the three chairs were tipped over.

---

[4] Joan Chittister, *Scarred by Struggle, Transformed by Hope*, (Grant Rapids, Michigan: William B Eerdmans Pub. Co., 2003), 83.

Total silence in the camp. On the horizon, the sun was setting.
'Caps off!' screamed the *Lageralteste*. His voice quivered. As for the rest of us, we were weeping.
'Cover your heads!'

Then came the march past the victims. The two men were no longer alive. Their tongues were hanging out, swollen and bluish. But the third rope was still moving: the child, too light, was still breathing...

And so he remained for more than half an hour, lingering between life and death, writhing before our eyes. And we were forced to look at him at close range. He was still alive when I passed him. His tongue was still red, his eyes not yet extinguished.

Behind me, I heard the same man asking:
'For God's sake, where is God?'
And from within me, I heard a voice answer:
'Where He is? This is where - hanging here from this gallows...'
That night, the soup tasted of corpses.
- *Night* by Elie Wiesel[5]


## Why do we suffer?

Let us start with the hard questions. How would you answer someone who asks you, 'Why are they suffering?' or 'Why does God allow suffering?' or 'What is God's response to suffering?' Or perhaps questions such as 'Why do the innocent suffer?' or 'Why have so many died before they had a chance to live?' or 'If God is good, why is there so much that seems bad?'

They are not easy questions to answer. In fact we may be the one who has asked them at difficult stages in our lives. So what happens when life doesn't work? Sooner or later we all have to deal with the issue of unjust suffering. Suffering can be manifested as physical pain, depression or anxiety, social isolation, or as spiritual or existential distress. People

---

[5] Elie Wiesel, *Night* (London: Penguin Books, 2006), 64-65.

suffer until the threat to one's inherent dignity is removed, or until they can accept and deal with it. In order to understand the best course of action in the midst of terrible anguish, it is important to read and explore a number of sources. In this chapter we will work through a Catholic understanding of suffering.

## Scripture and suffering

As we examine suffering, which is part and parcel of human life, though felt more acutely in times of injustice or during illness, ageing or nearing death, we are reminded of Gen 3:19, 'By the sweat of your face you shall eat bread until you return to the ground, for out of it you were taken; you are dust, and to dust you shall return.' However other Scriptural passages cast some faith filled light on understanding suffering.

Our first stop in reading through the Scriptures is the story of Jacob's wrestle with God found in Gen 32:23-32. In the story of Jacob's struggle, it describes the isolation, darkness, fear, powerlessness and vulnerability experienced. Joan Chittister writes, the spirituality of struggle, takes darkness and forms it into faith, takes one step beyond fear to courage, takes vulnerability and draws out of it the freedom that comes with self-acceptance, faces the exhaustion and comes to value endurance, touches the scars and knows them to be transformational.[6] The purpose of wrestling with the God of suffering, as we learn through the story of Jacob, is to reach a new sense of purpose in life.

Aside from Jacob's struggle where he limped away, yet for the better having gained insight, we enter into the story of 1 Kings 19, which is the encounter between the Prophet Elijah and God. Elijah's life was one of zealousness and faithfulness to God. Yet he soon enough found himself surrounded by enemies, imminent persecution and death. Elijah's reaction is to seek isolation. However fear and depression accompany him with death hovering overhead and the prospect of suffering before his eyes. Why go on when there appears to be no rewards in the struggle of

---

[6] Chittister, *Scarred by Struggle, Transformed by Hope*, 96.

life, as we discern from Elijah's call, 'I alone am left' (v10). It is the universal human cry of injustice and loneliness. Does life have any real meaning or is it best that the Lord, 'take it away' (v10)?

As Elijah wallows in self pity he is unexpectedly touched by the grace of God, for 'at his head was a cake baked on hot stones, and a jar of water. He ate and drank' (vv6-7). It is not the will of God that one should give up in times of distress, but rather God's promise urges us on. It is known that athletes reaching their limits in a marathon suddenly find that second wind to continue. Our spiritual life journey is something of the same. When life deals harsh blows there tends to be an inner strength, a resilience to keep going.

So Elijah, though downtrodden and unsure, turns in desperation to God. The struggle is not over, but the search for answers is in earnest. Elijah stands on Mount Horeb, alone, searching, wanting a response that will assure him all will be well. But first he must struggle with doubt and anger, as his world view seems to collapse before his very eyes. Elijah's current state of mind and heart reflected, 'a great wind, so strong that it was splitting mountains and breaking rocks in pieces before the Lord' (v11). Elijah is storm tossed, yet where is God? Only when Elijah can let go of the questions and seek God, can the confusion subsist and peace reign with 'a sound of sheer silence' (v12). Only then does Elijah overcome his fear of suffering and embraces the path ahead.

Our final Old Testament passage is the Book of Job. It puts forward profound questions about life after the collapse of Job's world of meaning, brought on by incomprehensible suffering. Job's friends were convinced that because of sin, Job had brought his sufferings upon himself and God had cast him off. Yet Job knows he does not deserve this tragedy and that God deserves his loyalty. The story unfolds with Job questioning and accusing God. It is about keeping faith in a God of justice when there appears to be no justice.

When God speaks to Job (ch 38-41), God neither reveals to Job why he is suffering, nor enters into the debate about the problem of evil. The relationship with God is more important than answers to our 'Why?' Through rhetorical questions, God forces Job to discern the wisdom in designing a creation of rhythms, paradoxes, order, changing patterns and limits.[7] Job's questions and God's speeches suggest that there is a gap between human comprehension and divine understanding. One's questioning is only answered through being placed in a wider context than human perception. The final outcome is that Job sees a vision of God who is victorious over all, realising the issue of any human situation can be safely left to God (42:2).

God's self-revelation of love allowed Jacob, Elijah and Job to know the meaning of life not through rational explanations but as encounter with God, realising that righteousness can exist alongside and even within tribulation. For Christians tossed around in relentless suffering, only the reality of a loving God can redeem their protests, doubts and exhaustion.

## Suffering, the Cross and Redemption

Our understanding of God in suffering is palpable in the New Testament where God becomes incarnate. Through Jesus we witness to a divine love that passes through human suffering and anguish in the Garden of Gethsemane (Mk 14:32-42), followed by crucifixion and death.

Jesus is fully aware that death is close at hand and tastes the suffering that will accompany him. He heads to the quiet space of the Garden to pray, to be alone and to gather his thoughts.

The disciples gather too. Jesus needs their reassuring company and in the presence of Peter, James and John, he 'began to be distressed and agitated' (v33). Emotions run amuck as one struggles to get their head

---

[7] Norman C. Habel, 'In defence of God the Sage' in *The Voice from the whirlwind: Interpreting the Book of Job* by Leo G Perdue and W. Clark Gilpin editors, (Nashville: Abingdon Press, 1992), 38.

around things and the body screams in defiance. Why is this happening? Jesus needs the reassurance, the comforting presence of friends, even though there may be no comforting words to voice. 'I am deeply grieved, even to death; remain here and keep awake' (v34). Jesus experienced deep distress and fell into the danger of despair as we witness on the Cross, 'Eloi, Eloi, lema sabachthani?' which means, 'My God, my God, why have you forsaken me?' (Mk 15:34). This cry of forsakenness eternally resounds as sufferers in every age experience the existential reality of forsakenness. As Dorothy Sayers writes:

> For whatever reason God chose to make man as he is – limited and suffering and subject to sorrows and death – He had the honesty and courage to take his own medicine. Whatever game he is playing with his creation, he has kept his own rules and played fair. He can exact nothing from man that he has not exacted for himself. He has himself gone through the whole of human experience, from the trivial irritations of family life and the cramping restrictions of hard work and lack of money to the worst horrors of pain and humiliation, defeat, despair, and death. When he was a man, he played the man. He was born in poverty and died in disgrace and thought it well worthwhile.[8]

If Jesus is 'the image of the invisible God' (Col 1:15) who is vulnerability is revealed on the cross (1 Cor 1:2-31), then our suffering is somehow one with God's suffering.

According to Pope John Paul II's document, *On the Christian meaning of human suffering,* the main question that arises within each form of suffering, be it psychological, physical, social or spiritual, is why do we suffer?[9] In looking at Christ, we have our answer and comfort for Christ shared in our humanity. Pope John Paul II elaborates, 'Christ drew

---

[8] Dorothy L. Sayers, *Christian Letters to a Post-Christian World* (Grand Rapids, Michigan: William B. Eerdemans Publishing Company, 1969), 14.
[9] Pope John Paul II. Apostolic Letter *Salvifici doloris* 11th Feb 1984. http://www.vatican.va/holy_father/john_paul_ii/apost_letters/documents/hf_jp-ii_apl_11021984_salvifici-doloris_en.html

close above all to the world of human suffering through the fact of having taken *this suffering upon his very self*... Precisely by means of his Cross he must accomplish *the work of salvation*. This work, in the plan of eternal Love, has a redemptive character.'[10] Human suffering has reached its culmination in the passion of Jesus and has entered into a new dimension, being linked to love.

The connection between the ministry of Jesus and his death on the cross is the ultimate expression of his commitment to give life to others. The centurion proclaims Jesus to be the Son of God, not because Jesus produced a miraculous feat, but because he saw how Jesus died a suffering, powerless death (Lk 23:47). We come to know Jesus best, through his passion, which symbolises his humanity, which is the real source of power. The encounter with suffering and death, when endured with courage and patience, and supported by others, can take on life-giving meaning, in the light of Jesus' suffering.

Redemption is about our own personal transformation into the likeness of Christ. We are transformed through suffering because it is in these times of trials and suffering one becomes aware of their fallen nature and their deep resistance to grace and the need for healing, hope and love.

## Reasons for suffering

Geoffrey Robinson lists reasons that religious communities have come up with in order to explain suffering. He also explains the problems with these responses.[11]

1. Suffering is a punishment for sin – a very ancient conviction. It simply does not fit the facts such as many bad people prosper and many good people suffer.

---

[10] Pope John Paul II. Apostolic Letter *Salvifici doloris* 11th Feb 1984, paragraph 16.
[11] Geoffrey Robinson, *Travels in Sacred Places*, (Blackburn, Victoria: Harper Collins Religious, 1997), 186.

2. Evil may prosper for a time but in the long run right will triumph – this is wishful thinking, an attempt to defend God rather than speak to the victims of suffering.

3. God has good reasons for all that happens. We see only the loose threads at the back but God sees the beautiful tapestry on the other side – God would be using people without their consent and often against their will.

4. Parents must often make their children do things they do not want to do. It is for their good. God does the same to us through suffering – parents never inflict pain solely so that children will learn to bear pain. If God were to do this, it would again be using people without their consent.

5. Suffering is sent as a test to strengthen us and God will never ask more of us than we can bear – but many people fail the test and are overwhelmed by their suffering.

6. Death releases us from the pain of this world – this is hardly an answer to the parents of a baby who has died. It is an attempt to do away with bad by calling it good.

These are responses to our false assumptions in the face of what often is unjust suffering. As we know from experience and the words of those who suffer, many people 'blame' God, or they may lose faith in a caring God, or choose to reason that it is punishment from God for one's sinfulness. Others may argue that it is part of God's plan. Yet how can a loving God purposefully will such pain and sorrow?

If one accepts that suffering is sent from God as a lesson, then one gives into resigned fatalism. Why should a person resist suffering if God has sent it to teach us a lesson? On the other hand one can learn to accept the good and bad as the following story tells: Arthur Ashe, the legendary Wimbledon player was dying of cancer. From the fans world over, he received letters, one of which conveyed, 'Why does God have to select you for such a bad disease?' To this Arthur Ashe replied, 'The world over –

about 50 million children start playing tennis, 5 million learn to play tennis, half a million learn professional tennis, 50,000 come to the circuit, 5000 reach the grand slam, 50 reach Wimbledon, 4 to semi finals, 2 to the finals. When I was holding a cup I never asked God 'Why me?' And today in pain I should not be asking, 'God why me?' Yet we do ask 'Why me?'

Richard Leonard provides seven steps to spiritual sanity when we are tempted to ask, 'Where the hell is God?'[12]

1. God does not directly send pain, suffering, and disease. God does not punish us.
2. God does not send accidents to teach us things, though we can learn from them.
3. God does not will earthquakes, floods, droughts, or other natural disasters. Prayer asks God to change us to change the world.
4. God's will is more in the big picture than in the small.
5. God did not need the blood of Jesus. Jesus did not come 'to die,' but God used his death to announce the end to death.
6. God has created a world that is less than perfect, and in which suffering, disease, and pain are realities; otherwise, it would be heaven. Some of these problems we create for ourselves and blame God.
7. God does not kill us off.

Despite differences in how individuals comprehend suffering, the Christian message is that God is involved. God became one of us, in Christ Jesus, to redeem, heal and offer meaning. By opening ourselves to the pain and tragedy of the world around us, we will grow beyond measured limits, and enter the depths of the mystery of this world. The value that emerges out of our life of contradiction is beautifully expressed

---

[12] Richard Leonard SJ, *Where the Hell is God?* (New Jersey: HiddenSpring, 2010), xvii.

in the poem, 'The Invitation' which was inspired by Oriah Mountain Dreamer, a Native American Elder, and written in 1994:

> . . . I want to know if you have touched the centre of your own sorrow, if you have been opened by life's betrayals or have become shrivelled and closed from fear of further pain! I want to know if you can sit with pain, mine or your own, without moving to hide it or fade it or fix it. I want to know if you can be with joy, mine or your own; if you can dance with wildness and let ecstasy fill you to the tips of your fingers and toes without cautioning us to be careful, be realistic, or to remember the limitations of being a human. . . I want to know if you can get up after the night of grief and despair, weary, bruised to the bone, and do what needs to be done for the children. It doesn't interest me who you are, how you came to be here. I want to know if you will stand in the centre of the fire with me and not shrink back. It doesn't interest me where or what or with whom you have studied. I want to know what sustains you from the inside, when all else falls away. I want to know if you can be alone with yourself; and if you truly like the company you keep in the empty moments.[13]

We cannot enter into the suffering of another if we have not accepted our own suffering. It is the invitation to come to awareness of our sinfulness and to encounter the mercy of God. Only then can we deeply understand and empathise with one another.

So when we are confronted with the question, 'Why did this happen to me?' perhaps we can, with genuine compassion, patiently walk with the person to a time when they can ask, 'How am I going to react to the suffering that has entered my life?' A pastoral care minister leads one to self acceptance in Christ, despite the present ambiguity faced. So let us end this chapter with an insight from Viktor E. Frankl, a survivor of the Holocaust, who writes:

---

[13] Oriah, 'Mountain Dreaming,' in *The Invitation,* (San Francisco: HarperONE, 1999).

... we had to teach the despairing men, that *it did not really matter what we expected from life, but rather what life expected from us*. . . Life ultimately means taking the responsibility to find the right answer to its problems and to fulfil the tasks which it constantly sets for each individual.[14]

---

[14] Viktor E. Frankl, *Man's search for Meaning*, (Boston: Beacon Press, 2006), 77.

# Chapter 3: Pastoral care as a response to human needs

> A deep encounter with the poor brings new life and a real meeting in which it is possible to discover that we too have hearts to love – and at the same time, we become aware of our fears and barriers: the search for comfort and security. If, once our hearts are touched, we allow ourselves to respond to the poor, we may gradually discover a power and hidden energy welling up from a deeper source than our knowledge and our capacity for 'doing.' We may also find an unsuspected ability to meet and serve others, thus becoming a sign of the love of God. We will find the strength of tenderness, goodness, patience, forgiveness, joy and celebration: a sealed spring bursting forth. - **Jean Vanier**[15]

What compels Christians to tenderly attend to the needs of others? It is surely more than State Law or the 'Good Samaritan Act.' One is compelled into service as a response to the movement of one's heart, the prick of their conscience, or through the loving bond they share with individuals.

The Scriptural passage Mt 25:31-46, is an imperative to serve. The emphasis here is on caring for one and all, with no distinction between race, gender or creed. As Paul writes, 'There is neither Jew nor Gentile, slave or free person, there is neither male nor female, for we are all one in Christ' (Gal 3:28). We are one Body in Christ and how we treat that body of living people is essential to our own well being and that of the entire community (1 Cor 12:12-27).

This understanding that we are all connected is evident. Jesus led the way with calling the lepers and outcasts back into society, in order to make the body of the people, whole again. In marriage vows, the promise is given to remain with each other in good and bad, in sickness and in

---

[15] Jean Vanier *A Door of Hope*. Translated by Teresa de Bertodano, (London: Hodder and Stoughton, 1996), 70.

health. In society corporate structures are established around the contribution of its members. Ultimately it is the deepening of bonds and strengthening of relationships that measure the true worth of individuals and the purpose of life. Until all are invited and all are accepted, we only achieve less than what can be entire. The full picture is an invitation to one and all.

## Tracing the historical development of the ministry of pastoral care

Jesus remains the perfect example of caring for people in any form of need and from this, pastoral care has always been at the heart of the Church's mission. Healing, guiding, sustaining and reconciling are the dominant characteristics of the practice of the Church. If we trace the development of the Church's mission to care, we see from the early beginning questions arose on how to respond to the Gentile converts to Christianity and the observance of Jewish Law. At the same time emphasis was placed on moral exhortation to help prepare for the return of the Lord in the Parousia.

During the next 250 years of the early Church, pastoral care entailed sustaining believers persecuted by the Roman State. Reconciling later dominated when Church and Empire opposed each other and problems arose over those who renounced their faith under threat of persecution and the terms on which they should be forgiven.

In the $5^{th}$ to $11^{th}$ centuries monasticism was valued. Penitentials of Celtic monks were sought as a way of reconciling. Pope Gregory the Great, wrote 'The Book of Pastoral Rule' at this time.

In the $12^{th}$ to $15^{th}$ centuries pastoral care was exercised through the healing power of sacraments, particularly Eucharist and Penance. There was a fear of damnation and a rise of devotional practices. Franciscan and Dominican Friars met spiritual and intellectual needs of the cities.
In the $16^{th}$ century, Catholic emphasis was on cultic priesthood and the importance of Mass and Confession. The priests were the pastoral

ministers and by the 17th & 18th centuries, they also took on the role of spiritual director.

The 19th century saw the emergence of the Industrial revolution and scientific developments. Social Action became the key word. By the late 20th Century, Vatican II (1962-1965) declared there existed a variety of ministries emerging among the laity. Prayer and spirituality were important in the role of pastoral care, but the most significant movement was the incorporation of social sciences and the realisation that global events have serious impact on the spiritual and pastoral life of believers. New pastoral concerns became medical technology, sexuality, environment, ageing, family changes, poverty and mental health.

The Church is empowered and guided by the Holy Spirit and all the baptised are invited to be witnesses to and live with the hopes and struggles of creation. As a Church they are called to be the ministers of God's presence and servants of the Kingdom, in fulfilment of the Gospel (Mk 16:15).

Thomas H. Groome identifies the components of Catholic ministry as the call to be an inclusive community of faith, hope and love that welcomes all people and engages each member's gifts 'for the life of the world' (*Koinonia*); to evangelise, preach and teach God's word of liberating salvation (*Kerygma*); to worship God publicly as an assembly of Christian people, celebrating God's covenant in Jesus Christ and the hope of salvation for all (*Leitourgia*); to care for human needs, spiritual, psychological, and physical and help build up God's reign of peace and justice in the world, with special favour for the poor and disadvantaged (*Diakonia*); and to bear credible public witness to Christian faith through lifestyle and example, even to the point of suffering and death (*Marturia*).[16] Ministry is pastoral because it engages concrete circumstances and emphasises community, compassion and conversion.

---

[16] Thomas H. Groome, *What makes us Catholic. Eight gifts for life* (NY: HarperSanFrancisco, 2002), 120.

## Defining pastoral care for today

Sometimes there is tension in regards to the aims of pastoral care. There are those who take the view that pastoral care must aim at conversion, leading the person more fully into the faith and life of the Church. Pastoral care is therefore understood as a form of evangelism or getting the person to receive the Sacraments.

The other model views pastoral relationship as non-judgmental, empathic, supportive and working towards getting the person to take greater self-responsibility. It is a ministry that arises from the conviction of faith within the carer to be a witness to Jesus' love for all.

Pastoral care includes helping people to grow psychologically and develop spiritually. It embraces both wholeness and holiness, leading people to full humanity through deeper self-acceptance and closer union with God. The role of the pastoral care giver includes being a creator of meaning, trustworthy listener, calming presence, generator of ethical concerns etc.

Yet the question arises, how does one get involved with a patient's moral dilemma without, on the one hand, agreeing with everything they say, or on the other hand, imposing one's views? Below is a personal insight into how even a great theologian such as Karl Rahner, experienced doubt as he undertook home visitations:

> O God, these people to whom you've thrown me out from my home with you! Mostly they won't accept me, your messenger, at all; they want nothing to do with your gifts, your grace, and your truth, with which you have sent me to them. . . And as for those who do let me in their houses that are their lives! They normally want anything but what I am meant to be bringing from you. They want to tell me about their wretched, tiny concerns; they want to pour out their hearts to me... And what do these people want of me? If it is not simply money, material help, or a little comfort from a sympathetic heart that they're seeking, they mostly look on me as some kind of insurance agent, with whom

they can take out a heavenly accident policy to prevent your breaking in upon their lives in the omnipotence of your holiness and justice, shaking them out of their tiny everyday concerns and their narrow Sunday self-satisfaction... How rarely does anyone want to confront the gift of your grace as it really is: tough, clear, not just for our consolation but also your glory, pure and upright, silent and bold.[17]

Karl Rahner asks the question, 'Am I the sort of messenger who just hands over your message and gift at the 'delivery entrance,' without ever being allowed to enter into the 'interior castle' of another's soul so as to be able to make sure that your message and your gift really becomes eternal life for this person through this person's free love.' He concludes, 'All care of souls – in its ultimate, true reality – is possible only in you, in your love that binds me to you and thus takes me with it also to the place to which you alone can still find a way: to human hearts.'[18]

The role of the pastoral care giver is to help the person find God's presence. Sometimes there may be an opportunity to help one to feel God's presence through prayer or hearing the Scriptures or participating in the Sacraments, however, pastoral care should be on their terms. It is a service that is personal, caring and compassionate.

Those entering pastoral care situations will need to deal not only with existential concerns as to the meaning of life (Why am I here? What is the meaning of my life? What happens when I die? Is there a benevolent God? Will I be forgiven? Why am I suffering?). There is also the encounter with abandonment, despair and hopelessness; anger that things are not right; questions as to God's presence and purpose; grief, guilt or shame; the need for reconciliation and to heal relationships; sense of isolation; and religious/spiritual struggles.

---

[17] Karl Rahner, 'God of my Sisters and Brothers,' in *Karl Rahner. Spiritual Writings*. Edited by Philip Endean, (Maryknoll: Orbis Books, 2004), 107-108.
[18] Rahner, 'God of my Sisters and Brothers,' 109-110.

The most general understanding of pastoral care is the communication of God's care for humankind as expressed in Jesus Christ. Pastoral care can be exercised by individuals, groups and communities. They can take on the roles of spiritual accompaniment, counsellor, companion, advocate, theologian and ethicist. Some of the kinds of life situations that can be helped by pastoral care include crisis care, family and marriage counselling, supportive care for the dying and bereaved, spiritual direction, drug addiction therapy, moral decision making, care of the sick, sexual issues and general loss of meaning and value in life. Jean Vanier provides a visual image of pastoral care:

> I love the image of the wounded bird held in the cupped hand. The hand is not too open, otherwise the bird might fall. It is not too closed door that might crush the bird. The hand is like a nest. It carries and gives support to the bird, communicating warmth and security to him so that when the right moment comes, he can regain strength and take off on his own. The father is like this cupped hand. He does not possess the child; he does not enclose him nor harm him, but he helps the child so that later, he may take off on his own. Our lives, our bodies, our communities, are called to be this cupped hand in order to receive and carry others. Not to possess, harm, judge, or condemn them, but to carry them. To carry the weakest ones with their suffering, anger, depression, dreams, illusions, and lack of confidence as well as their light, hope, and possibility for growth. We are called to carry them until they can take off on their own, and become more completely themselves, capable of choosing their new home.[19]

Elaine Graham explains that a therapeutic model of Church emphasizes as its key activity the practice of personal care, support and healing. The primary locus of such a model is upon the interpersonal encounter, the intimacies of listening, conversation and solicitous concern. The theological dimensions to this model lie in its emphasis on the implicit values of healing and reconciliation.[20]

---

[19] Jean Vanier, *A Door of Hope*, 44.
[20] Elaine L. Graham, *Words made flesh. Writings in pastoral and practical Theology*, (London: SCM Press, 2009), 148.

Psychologists have classified human needs according to different categories. Abraham Maslow (1943) provides a classification, known as the 'Hierarchy of Human Needs.' The five basic needs are physiological, safety, love, esteem and self-actualisation. For Maslow, the lower order needs (physiological and safety) are dominant until satisfied, where upon the higher order needs come into operation. Since the average adult in Australian culture is largely satisfied in their lower needs, physiological and safety needs do not act as motivators. Therefore, the higher needs emerge of love, belonging and esteem, which when satisfied lead to self-confidence, worth and capability in the world. The final basic need is self-actualisation, which is the desire to become more of what one is capable of becoming.

So pastoral care of the person is a response to the needs for warmth, nurture, support and care. These needs are heightened during times of personal stress and social chaos. Sin and salvation, alienation and reconciliation, guilt and forgiveness, judgment and grace, spiritual death and rebirth, despair and hope, are interwoven in the interaction between carer and patient.

## Generic chaplaincy - just spiritual care?

Charles Taylor refers to secularity within the heritage of Latin Christendom in three related but distinct ways.

1. As the expulsion of religion from public institutions and practices;

2. As the decline in public belief and worship (falling church attendance);

3. As a change in the context and social attitude toward belief.

This third category concerns the shift from a society where belief in God was effectively present in all social interactions, to one in which faith has become one option among many.[21]

Fewer people today express their spirituality through participation in rituals and it has become increasingly awkward to raise religious matters in public life. The lessening of orthodox religious expression has generated a greater need for chaplaincy that is self-aware, open to the experiences of others, and able to articulate a theology of practical relevance.[22]

H. Tristram Engelhardt raises the question in regards to generic chaplaincy in hospitals. Such chaplaincy is religion non specific and denominationally neutral. It provides spiritual care to any denomination and people of any faith, if called upon. Yet what assumptions are made about the nature of spiritual care and about the significance of religion? Furthermore what do we do about ecumenical views, truth claims and religious commitments? Generic chaplains are seen as part of a healthcare team rather than a service and mission. The focus as Engelhardt puts it, 'is no longer on providing care from the richness of a particular religion, but rather on transcending religious or denominational boundaries to reach out to anyone in spiritual need.'[23] Does this suggest that spiritual care is no longer taken seriously in the salvation of patients or that salvation is not taken seriously as an important element in the patient's well being? Furthermore can one argue about inadequate spiritual care?

The type of spiritual care offered in a pluralistic, multicultural setting is often watered down to the lowest common denominator. Severed from

---

[21] Christopher Swift, *Hospital Chaplaincy in the Twenty-first Century*, (England: Ashgate, 2009), 127.
[22] Swift, *Hospital Chaplaincy in the Twenty-first Century*, 135, 144.
[23] H. Tristram Jr., 'Generic chaplaincy: providing spiritual care in a post-Christian age' in (*Christian Bioethics* 4, no.3, 1998), 233.

religion, it is often devoid of content and 'domesticate the spirit.'[24] Generic spirituality may speak to all people but as Stephen Pattison writes, 'such a sterile, non-located area of concern may have little of value and substance to offer, least of all those who face problems of life and death.'[25]

The spiritual dimension of a person contributes to self esteem, a sense of purpose, and a set of goals and objectives in life.[26] So in times of illness and suffering, when moral and ethical are at play, the authority of Scripture, religious teachings and beliefs, rituals and spiritual practices, all have an important role to play in an individual's path towards healing and acceptance.

Research has shown that patients do want their physicians and nurses to address spiritual issues, along with spiritual support from their religious chaplains. There is obviously nothing generic about health and sickness, well-being and suffering.

## Christian pastoral care

A Catholic perspective views pastoral care as healing of body and soul, through Scripture, Sacraments and acts of love. It considers care that include cultural, spiritual and religious dimensions.

Pastoral care offers consolation and healing presence which comes from God and which supports one in all situations of life, including the

---

[24] Abigail Rian Evans, 'Healing in the Midst of Dying: A Collaborative Approach to End-of-Life Care' in *Living well and dying Faithfully*, John Swinton and Richard Payne (ed), (Grand Rapids, Michigan: William B. Eerdmans Publishing Company, 2009), 167.

[25] Stephen Pattison, *The challenge of Practical Theology. Selected Essays* (London: Jessica Kingsley Publishers, 2007), 138.

[26] Evans, 'Healing in the Midst of Dying: A Collaborative Approach to End-of-Life Care,' 185.

sick and dying. In Christian spiritual tradition the gift of the Spirit that the pastoral carer awakens the patient too, entails meaning, transformation, encounter and healing.

Competent witness of religious faith is called for. Thus prayer, worship and ritual, provide a way of working with and for God, that is lacking in the generic quest to meet spiritual needs which tends to be individualistic, introspective, personal and quietistic.'[27]

Spiritually sensitive carers do not rationalize away the patient's confusion but rather ask questions and seek understanding through that process. Sufferers have to slowly learn new ways of seeing the world and new patterns of emotional behaviour. Even if specific answers are not found, patients can come to an acceptance of being with the unknown. In uncertainty, suffering and disillusionment, we recall the words of Christ to Julian of Norwich, 'But all shall be well, and all manner of things shall be well.'[28]

In the midst of suffering, a skilful and compassionate person can be an important anchor in which the patient can find solace and move through distress to inner peace.

The pastoral care minister is someone who cannot only be deeply affected by the feelings and troubles of others, but who also shares their plight. Personal concern means making the patient the one who counts, the one we leave everything for. One enters the situation with hope, enters the experience with vision, and enters into communion, seeking restoration. Ray Anderson discovered, 'The art of caregiving is more a matter of being tuned to the spirit rather than pressing the correct keys on

---

[27] Pattison, *The challenge of Practical Theology. Selected Essays*, 141.
[28] Julian of Norwich, *Revelations of Divine Love*, (London: Penguin Books, 1998), 22.

an instrument... when spiritual doors are open, the Spirit of God breathes once again the gift of life into our mortality.'[29]

Pastoral care practice includes respect for the individual as a person and acceptance of the person as they are, along with their priorities and values. The care offered is to enable the person to regain, maintain and develop their integrity as the persons they were created to be, with a sense of self-responsibility. Given the opportunity to enter deep into their sacred space, the pastoral carer is able to encourage the other to speak their truth, fears, anguish and hopes and to share in the growth and peace that can emerge.

---

[29] Ray S Anderson, *Spiritual Caregiving as Secular Sacrament. A Practical Theology for Professional Caregivers* (London: Jessica Kingsley Publishers, 2003), 178.

# Chapter 4: Pastoral care qualities

> Isn't all our dread a dread of being just here? Of being only this? Of having no other thing to become? Of having nowhere to go really but where we are? - **Kenneth Patchen**[30]

When dealing with the most fundamental and important issues of life, the great mysteries of being and nonbeing, of source and destiny, of value and morality, of the nature of suffering and pain, they are best approached with faith, hope and love are needed for those 'who labour and are heavy burdened'.

## What to avoid in pastoral care

In our care of others there are some words and actions that are best not used! Below are a few suggestions to refrain from, some we hope quite obvious! A number have been suggested by Jill McGilvray.[31]

Blaming, criticising or judging
Advice giving, moralising or preaching
Interpreting situations for the person out of your own frame of reference
Denying or arguing with their version of reality
Interrupting to reassure, comfort and console
Saving or rescuing
Fidgeting or watching the time
Finishing their sentences
Telling them what to feel or think
Insisting the person talk about their loss

---

[30] Maxie Dunman, *The workbook on Coping as Christians*, (Tennessee: The Upper Room, 1993), 85.
[31] Jill McGilvray, *God's love in action. Pastoral Care for everyone* (Victoria: Acorn Press, 2009), 47.

Rush the person out of their illness
Suggest miracle cures
Imply lack of prayer or faith
Offer comfort with such words as, 'It's OK' as it is not okay for them
Saying 'I know just how you feel' because you do not
'It must have been God's will' because one will ask why would God wants such suffering
'At least it's not as bad as…'
'It's for the best'
'At least you have your faith' assumes the person is ok with it all, when they may really be questioning the goodness of God.

## What is recommended in pastoral care

Pastoral care involves a commitment of time and energy, ongoing training and accountability. Hurting people need validation, normalisation, empathy, time and privacy. So below are a few suggestions:

Gently enquire after them
Listen
Be prepared to hear the story over and over again
Acknowledge what the loss means for the person
Sitting alongside them with love and patience
Provide practical help such as meals, grocery shopping, gardening etc
Send a heartfelt message/card
Visit someone homebound and maybe with a bunch of flowers or food. . .
Invite them to something they may enjoy such as a concert etc
Offer to read to someone whose eye sight is failing
Provide a pleasant experience such as a car drive, coffee etc
Offer to baby sit for a few hours
Pray with and for the person
Be a guide to seeking and understanding God's perspective
Encourage the person to seek further counsel if need be
Be supportive

Accept feelings no matter what they are or how unusual they appear
Maintain predictability and stability in the environment
Accept silences without filling them with words
Use physical touch if acceptable when words seem inappropriate
Encourage expression of emotion
Ask the hard questions with gentleness
Follow up and stay for the long haul
Adopt an empathetic attitude

We witness to the noble human spirit during heartaches. People share their griefs and stories, bring extra food for their neighbours, open their homes to offer shelter, donate thousands of goods, strangers hug one another in an attempt to comfort, people cry together, and many volunteer their services and time. It becomes obvious, when we witness and hear to such actions, that offering pastoral care is an inherent ability. What follows are four particular characteristics that pastoral carers should cultivate in themselves.

## Faith

If it is faith in Jesus that bears us along in our trials, then let us take a closer look. Jesus was a fool's Messiah riding into Jerusalem on an ass as a scapegoat saviour. That is how Jesus approached his life and chose to face the suffering he was soon to endure, rather than play to the political and ecclesiastical kingdoms of earth. We in our Christian faith therefore must understand that when there is a violation of our normal conceptual patterns and expectations, which occurs in suffering, our faith carries us through that emotional disengagement. Jesus confounded human reason and that is the faith that allows us to endure our suffering.

In accepting the non permanence of life, one pursues their faith prepared for the unexpected and extraordinary. They become open minded people. It is faith in the very things that are impossible that gives one a spirituality of suffering unlike anyone else.

Faith in the impossible allows one to possess the qualities of love, loyalty, watchfulness and courage which would seem otherwise impossible in suffering. In suffering, faith calls one to be like the Canaanite woman who fell to her knees before Jesus, to 'eat the crumbs that fall from the master's table' before the master will say, 'great is your faith!' (Mt 15:21-26). This blind faith always gives the Christian a spirit to soar above all that darkens.

To have faith even in suffering and darkness, represents the capacity to enjoy the whole of life regardless of the fortunes of one's existence. One learns how to devalue the valuable and revalue the supposedly valueless, learning to take pleasure in simple and common things.

## Hope

Hope has been scientifically proven to contribute significantly to the healing of people not only from mental or spiritual illness, but also from physical illness. It is a hope that is grounded in the living God, who is Creator and Saviour.[32]

The Christian hope is in a loving God and belief that one's life is heading for eternal fulfilment. To achieve hope involves a balance between emotional support to prevent self-destruction and encouraging the person to accept responsibility for their situation, despite fragility, illness and brokenness.

Hope is a matter of putting one foot in front of the other when we can find no reason to do so. As Joan Chittister explains, we dispel despair with hope, but it takes effort. Hope takes life on its own terms, knows that whatever happens God lives in it, and expects that, whatever its twists and turns, it will ultimately yield its good to those who live it consciously.[33]

---

[32] Evans, 'Healing in the Midst of Dying: A Collaborative Approach to End-of-Life Care,' 179.
[33] Chittister, *Scarred by Struggle, Transformed by Hope*, 106.

In times of misfortune, those with hope are neither steeped in self-pity, bemoaning their fate, nor do they berate themselves with self-blame or regret. Instead they get on with their lives.[34] This is something we work towards as the Pope writes:

> Suffering as it were, contains a special call to the virtue which one must exercise on their own part. And this is the virtue of perseverance in bearing whatever disturbs and causes harm. In doing this, the individual unleashes hope, which maintains in one the conviction that suffering will not get the better of them, that it will not deprive them of their dignity as a human being, a dignity linked to awareness of the meaning of life.'[35]

A sense of hope in suffering allows one to see things as part of a bigger picture, while learning to gauge the relative importance of things. One in suffering no longer fears or overlooks the imperfect and fragmented forms that occur, but the hopeful and optimistic solution is to go beyond all such distinctions. One becomes capable of handling dark and painful situations in more ways than one.

With the spirituality of hope one can stand apart from a situation, no matter how emotional, tense or negatively charged it may be, and divert their energies. Hope will insist on affirming, renewing and delighting in life without being so overwhelmed. Hope can express a certain heroic defiance in the face of life's defeats, displaying an unquenchable nobility of spirit that neither permits a given fate nor oppressor to have the last word nor to be absolute.

The virtue of hope springs forth from the exuberance of life itself, no matter who seeks to destroy the spirit. This is vividly depicted in the award winning Italian film, 'Life is Beautiful'. It is an amazing story of the struggle of one Jewish man to maintain hope for his young son, in the

---

[34] Carlo Notaro, *Comedy, Tragedy and Religion*, (New York, State University of New York Press, 1999), 17.
[35] Pope John Paul II, *On the Christian Meaning of Human Suffering*, 13.

midst of the horrific holocaust. Such hope creates a quality of soul that inspires others. So the virtue of hope in the spirituality of suffering then is to maintain the desire for goodness in life, despite the surrounding circumstances.

## Love

Love will give in to tears but not to despair. Love in suffering moves from playful innocence, through truth and justice, to humility and compassion. We are called to honour others, refusing to allow anything to separate us from the love and healing of Christ.

The virtue of love seeks to be part of the struggle for justice of the powerless, empathizing with those suffering. As Dunman puts it, 'in love's service only the wounded soldier can serve.'[36] One comes to possess through life's experiences, a love that helps them overcome one's suffering while allowing one to minister spiritually to those who suffer.

How many times do we hear of people who regret not having expressed their love to the dying person or count themselves at peace because they were able to tell their dying friend how much they loved them? Though in tragedy one may enter into alienation, guilt, rage and horror, one through love in suffering, particularly at the dying moments, restores balance and a renewed sense of dignity and justice. Love opens up both the sufferer and the bereaved to sympathy and goodwill, including one another in their generosity. Notaro explains that we must be a source of Christ's healing love to those who suffer. A love that listens to the heart and shares the mystery of life is the way to minister to the one that suffers.[37] We become fools blinded by love for God and life. Hope and faith both lead to love that aids both the sufferer and the minister.

---

[36] Dunman, *The workbook on Coping as Christians*, 99.
[37] Carlo Notaro, 'Ministering to the dying: Passage through fear, guilt and grief' in *Camillianum* 6(1995), 253.

## Presence

Loren Townsend explains that pastoral presence, 'is closely tied to biblical and theological images of God whose presence sustains creation and Christ's incarnation in the world. Pastoral presence is experienced in an emotional joining that allows 'true connection' with clients, 'understanding deeply from the heart,' or believing for clients when they cannot themselves believe. Often counselling sessions are referred to as 'holy ground' on which the client and counsellor become 'co-pilgrims on a spiritual journey.'[38]

There is a story about a child wanting to be held by his mother at bedtime. When the mother reminded the little boy that the arms of God would be around him all night, the child replied, 'I know, but tonight I need a God with skin on.' There are times when all of us need a God with skin on. Everything that we know in our minds must somehow come through the channels of our senses. If we are to be church then I know that I need you, to stand next to me, a God with skin. I need to hear your voice being raised with mine in prayer. I need to know by the experience of your nearness that God has made you my sister, my brother, and that we are together God's family. God reaches out to me through you and out to you through me.[39]

A pastoral carer's presence can offer much by way of encouragement, conversation, assistance and hope. Henri Nouwen describes the carer and the patient as two people 'who reawaken in each other the deepest human intuition, that life is eternal and cannot be made futile by a biological process.'[40]

---

[38] Loren Townsend, *Introduction to Pastoral Counselling*, (Nashville: Abingdon Press, 2009), 108-109.
[39] John Powell with Michael H Cheney, *A Life-Giving Vision: How to be a Christian in Today's world* (Allen, Texas: Thomas More Publishing, 1995).
[40] Henri J. M. Nouwen, *The Wounded Healer. Ministry in Contemporary Society*, (New York: Image Books Doubleday, 1979), 63, 69.

Unconditional presence is about being available for dialogue not indoctrination. Michael E. Cavanagh writes that the quality of being 'unconditionally' present means that whatever decisions people make and however far from the Kingdom their paths wander, the effective minister will always be at their side, attempting to shed light and bring assistance.[41] While caregivers may not be able to bring rational coherence to the experience, one can be fully present, even as they are only partially able to enter the lived experience of the person.

## Compassion

The Hebrew Scriptures use two terms to describe God: *hesed*, often translated as 'loving kindness,' and *rachum*, meaning 'compassion.' God relates to us with great compassion. The English word compassion comes from the Latin words *com* and *passus* meaning *to suffer with*. Both words carry a sense that God goes the extra mile for everyone, with added favour toward those who need it most.

Compassion, similar to empathy, is the ability and willingness to bear suffering alongside the other. It is about full immersion into the condition of being human. When a mother has lost her child, there is no way of dispelling her grief, but one can be there, with compassion, as a loving friend to support and encourage her. It is about remaining present to that person, while doing nothing, but with a heart filled with gift of hope of the Holy Spirit. In seeing the misfortunes of others, a mature Christian passes over into mercy.

In looking at the qualities of pastoral care, we become aware that empathising is important and that feelings, the emotions of the heart, need to be carefully attended to. As Joan D Chittister writes in *Heart of Flesh*:

---

[41] Michael E Cavanagh, *The Effective Minister: Psychological and Social Considerations*, (San Francisco: Harper and Rowe, 1986), 30.

When poets talk about the human soul, they do not talk about the reason; they talk about feeling. The totally human human being, they enable us to see, is the one who weeps over evil, revels in goodness, loves outrageously, and carries the pain of the world in healing hands. Feeling is the mark of saints. It is Vincent de Paul tending the poor on the back streets of France, Mother Teresa with a dying beggar in her arms, Florence Nightingale tending the wounded in the midst of battle, John the apostle resting trustingly on the breast of Jesus, Damian binding the running sores of lepers on the island of Molokai, the soup-kitchen people in our own towns giving hours of their lives, week after fruitless week, to feed the undernourished children, the homeless women, and the down-and-outs of both the U.S. and Canada, among the richest countries on the earth. Feeling, we know deep within us, signals the real measure of a soul. . . Feelings lead us to the people who love us through life and satisfy our souls when nothing else about a situation can sustain us at all. Feelings, devoid of thought, made only of mist, become the inner lights that lead us out of harm's way and home to our better selves. Feeling leads us to love the God we cannot see and to see the God around us whom we have yet to come to love.[42]

## Prayer

In turning to Scripture we discover comfort in knowing that even Jesus felt 'sorrow and distress' and asked his Father, 'if it is possible, let this cup pass from me, yet not as I will, but as you will' (Mt 26:36). As Christians we need to find the courage to confront the things we must change and to accept the things we cannot. This can only be achieved when we learn the prayer of healing that hears our cry for help and provides hope and strength for our life's journey.

Often this prayer will be a torrent of anguished questions to God as expressed by Pope John Paul II, 'For man does not put this question to the world, even though it is from the world that suffering comes to him,

---

[42] Joan D Chittister, *Heart of Flesh*, (Grand Rapids, Michigan: William B. Eerdmans Publishing Company, 1998), 50.

but he puts it to God as Creator and Lord of the world.'[43] One discovers that when they persist in prayer, they learn to give themselves over to the Father, believing that Jesus' example, teaching and presence through the Spirit, can affect their life positively.

Prayer can be a time when Jesus provides that nurturing, healing touch which frees and empowers one to lovingly touch others and heal. Prayer remains a universal answer. God has promised to deliver, heal, renew and energize us.

In 1 Thess 5:17 we read, 'Pray without ceasing.' A pastoral carer may offer the person the ability to pray. Yet the person seeking care may resist. This is because it involves struggle, negotiating danger, coping with pain, trying to achieve some sort of security, and being assured. Questions are asked that must be answered, experiences are remembered that must be faced. But through conversation and the gentle presence of the pastoral carer, reassurance can take place, answers can arise, and hope embraced. Others in pain often lose the ability to form thoughts into sentences and find praying hard. Therefore the pastoral carer can provide words to their needs and help hand the problem over to God.

Prayer is intended to bring one into accord with God's will, equipping one to face problems by encouraging a change of heart, which medicine alone cannot do. It leads others to an openness to God and an acceptance of life's challenges with the knowledge that God is in control (Rm 8:31). Often the answers to prayer may lead not to physical healing but the healing of broken relationships or reconciliation with a loved one.[44]

Traditional prayer forms such as the Lord's Prayer, the rosary or novenas, can be valuable resource in pastoral care. However they can also

---

[43] Pope John Paul II, *On the Christian Meaning of Human Suffering,* (Boston: Pauline Books and Media, 1984), 13.

[44] Evans, 'Healing in the Midst of Dying: A Collaborative Approach to End-of-Life Care,' 183.

be a defence against intimacy with God. The basis for prayer is that which is of the moment, existential and dialogical. Prayer should be used to affirm the presence of God and to inspire hope in patients who are worried, anxious, or feeling guilty, and in families who are grieving. Prayer alleviates patients' anxiety and sustains them through crisis, by sharing their concerns with God. Prayer is an instrument of healing.

Alan Paton in *For You, Departed* writes many years after the death of his wife, 'something within me is waking from long sleep, and I want to live and move again. Some zest is returning to me, some immense gratefulness for those who love me, some strong wish to love them also.'[45] Therefore one prays so that they can forgive and continue on with life no matter the struggle.

## Conclusion

As imperfect humans, our lives will involve falls, reversal of fortune, or suffering of some sort or other. Nevertheless it can be a redeeming experience when the pastoral care giver can offer faith, hope, love, presence, compassion and prayer. Faith becomes hope in foolishness and hope is able to take a positive attitude through misfortunes which otherwise leaves one feeling inadequate and helpless. So the spirituality of suffering is embraced with a love that becomes a minister to all that needs healing. Along with presence, compassion and prayer, faith, hope and love are essential in a spirituality of suffering, for they give meaning to go on.

---

[45] Maxie Dunman, *The workbook on Coping as Christians*, (Nashville, Tennessee, The Upper Room, 1993), 121.

# Chapter 5: Pastoral care to the young

'In Louisville, at the corner of Fourth and Walnut, in the centre of the shopping district, I was suddenly over whelmed with the realization that I loved all those people, that they were mine and I theirs, that we could not be alien to one another even though we were total strangers. It was like waking from a dream of separateness, of spurious self-isolation in a special world, the world of renunciation and supposed holiness... There is no way of telling people that they are walking around shining like the sun.' - **Thomas Merton**

Young people seek some sort of meaningful stability in a myriad of ever changing fast paced living. So let us take a closer look at our younger generations.

## Generations Y and Z

Generation Y are those born between 1980 and 1995. Generation Z are born in 1996 onwards. For these generations personal experience confirms truth. They expect instant communication and constant connection, are technologically and multimedia savvy, seek constant entertainment and have access to excess, are interactive with information and intellectually open, they desire to do something for the common good, are accepting and tolerant of diversity, and are over busy and over committed.

For young Australians they also experience a society characterized by cultural plurality, consumerism, unemployment rates, increasing housing costs, body image, crime rates, cyber bullying, loneliness and isolation, addictions, family issues, poverty, sexuality, pressure and despair about the future. Richard Eckersley comments about youth in modern Western Culture:

> The following three features of modern Western culture – our chosen individual, secular and material values, the rate and complexity of change, and the lack of a shared vision of society and its future – all tend to isolate individuals from each other and from society... Modern Western culture is increasingly failing to meet the basic requirements of any culture, which are to provide people with a sense of meaning, belonging and purpose and so a sense of personal identity, worth and security, a measure of confidence or certainty about what the future holds for them, and a framework of moral values to guide their conduct.[46]

As young people find themselves in a western worldview characterized by individualism and secularism, family and friendships become critical and the school world and internet world also play a large role in their lives. *The Spirit of Generation Y* (2003-2006), found these young people relied on family and friends as the source of their beliefs, values and social support. Secularization, consumer capitalism and individualism, were also significant in shaping their contemporary religion and spirituality.[47]

## Young people today

Common to humanity is the longing for something more. Some examples include a need for purpose, a sense of loneliness, a desire to be loved, or a thirst to feel valued or significant. Being in a positive environment and with people who are accepting, supportive, and able to effectively address questions during that searching phase, is essential for young people.

Youth pastoral care is realised through a network or cooperative activities in schools, parishes, families and the local community. It is important for young people to realise that they belong to a family that is much bigger than their current experience. As pastoral care givers of the

---

[46] Richard Eckersley, 'Values and visions: youth and the failure of modern Western Culture' in *Youth Studies* Vol. 14, No. 1, Autumn 1995.

[47] Michael Mason, Andrew Singleton, Ruth Webber, *The Spirit of Generation Y. Young People's spirituality in a changing Australia,* (Victoria: John Garret Publishing, 2007), 69.

young, opportunities need to be provided for youth to discuss pressing issues and is vital to their development as confident young people.

In the attribute, 'Such a Strange Mixture' the anonymous author depicts the inner yearnings of young Australians.

> I'm such a strange mixture God: Something greater than human wisdom is needed to sort me out and make me whole. Some days I soar, like an eagle over the peaks of the Great Divide, yet on other days I'm like a cockroach hiding in dark places. Sometimes, like a surfer at Coolangatta I truly enjoy riding life's rough waves, but at other times I just sit and complain, allowing the surf to break over me, filling my eyes with grit, and my soul with self-pity. There are special moments of prayer when I beg you to take me hiking among the mountain places of the Spirit, followed by pessimistic moods when my bleating prayers rise no higher than ant hills. God you have searched me and known me. You know the strange mixture that hides behind my public face. Take me in hand. Be to me not the God I want but the God I need.

This prayer is a gentle reminder that life experience has its ups and downs and young people are searching not only for answers but a sense of belonging, a spiritual encounter that offers hope and comfort, healing and security, assurance and wonder. Pastoral care creates networks of support for young people, communities and families.

## Pastoral care of the young

As caregivers we provide young people with support, guidance, compassionate care, accurate information, and confrontation when necessary. Other ways to engage with young people include:-
Discuss ways for being successful beyond educational, career and financial success;
Talk about role models;
Encourage an atmosphere where young people can communicate their hopes;

Encourage flexibility, creativity, engagement, reflection; Life testimonies;
Discussion in classrooms and on campuses;
Prayer;
Empower young people into leadership positions;
Meet them where they are – visit, affirm, invite;
Provide space where they can feel comfortable being open;
Adapt to different cultures;
Empathize with them;
Be supportive;
Be positive;
Be genuinely interested in them;
Talk over their ideas and views;
Always listen to what they say; and
Develop trust. It is about ongoing relationship with young people.

One-on-one dialogue with young people allows them to express what is really below the surface and allows them to discover that their issues are shared by others as well. This provides opportunities to connect and offer genuine discussion and care. It leads to building relationships and offers time for them to reflect on what can be done to achieve things. The settings in which pastoral ministry can be carried out with young people include a range of contexts from families, church, school or university, libraries, clubs, sporting teams etc.

We hear the phrase that young people today have everything, want everything and demand everything. Yet they also experience broken families, violence, addiction etc. So can they have too much of love, understanding, friendships etc. In pastoral we challenge and confront negative or harmful behaviours, values and attitudes, and invite the young to witness to positive values and lifestyles. Pastoral care with the young may also require collaboration with social services, community resources, and educational and governmental organizations.

## Chapter 6: Pastoral care to the sick

As institutions, hospitals can no more bring real healing to persons than churches can heal souls. Healing is a spark of the divine carried in earthen vessels. But people - physicians, nurses, chaplains, faith-filled families – may bring about cures and participate significantly in the drama of healing, not in hospitals or churches as institutions, but inasmuch as they become real communities; not as doctors or clergy in their capacity as technicians, but inasmuch as they become true healers, and a community of caring and respectful strangers. - **Anthony J. Gittins**[48]

Pastoral care could be very influential, inviting and involving medical administrators and promoting marriages between institutional efficiency and human compassion. But this requires Western society with all its scientific and technical expertise to ensure that where there is suffering grace may also abound, and where there is knowledge, wisdom also flourishes. Doctors and ministers must show their human face and human feelings and to be an integral part of the community that suffers, and not simply outsiders sent to redeem it. Our redeemer took on our suffering and *became as we are*. - **Anthony J. Gittins**[49]

## Religion as beneficial - Studies

During our life we often struggle, feel depressed, are under economic, moral, physical or relational pressure or facing suffering of some other sort. All this impacts on our health, which can endanger the physical-psychic-spiritual interrelationship of our daily living.[50] It therefore is not surprising that we are all in search for ways to cope with life.

---

[48] Gittins, *Reading the Clouds. Mission Spirituality for New Times*, 88.
[49] Gittins, *Reading the Clouds. Mission Spirituality for New Times*, 90-91.
[50] Carlo Notaro, 'Experience and concepts of health' in *Camillianum Magazine: International Magazine for Pastoral Theology of Healthcare*, 90

Research reveals that religious involvement, personal faith, and spirituality, have positive effects for a majority of people who turn to religious resources to cope with life stress, personal loss, natural disaster, war, mental and physical illness, and other problems.[51]

Results of more than 200 published studies of religion's impact on physical health show the positive effect of religious involvement, whether this is measured by religious attendance, belief in God, religious experience, or frequent prayer. James Gollnick suggests how Religion may produce these salutary effects in a variety of ways:[52]

- Religious commitment is usually associated with lower rates of deleterious behaviours, such as smoking, drinking and drug abuse;
- Religious participation can act as a social support network;
- Religious worship and prayer engender positive emotional experiences, such as relaxation, hope, forgiveness and love;
- Religious faith may lead to optimism about one's health, trusting that God will look after all aspects of life;
- Religious worldviews are significantly correlated with health.

Clinical trials show religious intervention produces faster results in reducing clinical mental health symptoms than therapies that exclude them and may be linked to religion promoting a positive worldview, helping clients make sense of difficult situations and providing purpose and meaning.

---

[51] Loren Townsend, *Introduction to Pastoral Counselling*, (Nashville: Abingdon Press, 2009), 117.
[52] James Gollnick, *Religion and Spirituality in the Life Cycle*, (NY: Peter Lang, 2008), 217.

## Catholic Health Care in Australia

The healing ministry of Christ is an integral part of the Church's mission. Catholic Health Australia is the largest non-government provider grouping of health, community and aged care services in Australia for over 160 years. Its commitment and service provision include aged care, disability services, family services, paediatric, children and youth services, mental health services, palliative care, alcohol and drug services, veterans' health, primary care, acute care, non acute care, step down transitional care, rehabilitation, diagnostics, preventative public health, medical and bioethics research institutes.[53] A snapshot of the Catholic Health and Aged Care Sector reveals:

- 19,000 residential aged care beds
- 6,253 retirement and independent living units and serviced apartments
- 8,000 Community Aged Care packages (CACP)
- 6,000 Home and Community Care programs (HACC) and Extended Aged Care at Home packages (EACH)
- rural and regional aged care facilities and services
- 9,500 beds in 75 health care facilities - publicly (21) and privately (54) funded hospitals
- 7 teaching hospitals
- 8 dedicated hospices and palliative care services
- expanding day centres and respite centres
- approximately 35,000 people working in the sector.[54]

---

[53] Catholic Health Australia http://www.cha.org.au/site.php?id=24
[54] Catholic Health Australia http://www.cha.org.au/site.php?id=24

The Code of ethics for Catholic Social Services Australia 2006, describes the purpose of the mission as:

> CSSA's vision is for a society in which there is full recognition of individual rights and responsibilities; a society that promotes the dignity, equality and participation of all persons.[55]

As pastoral carers from a Catholic tradition, one is called to attend to the needs of neighbour, particularly the sick, disabled, frail or elderly. One works to recover health and encourage participation in the life of family, church and wider society, as well as providing for people's spiritual and sacramental needs.

## Hospital chaplaincy

In Australia there are a number of Hospital Chaplaincy Boards, including Health Care Chaplaincy, Australian Chaplaincy - the Health Care Chaplains Council of Victoria (HCCVI) and the Civil Chaplaincy Advisory Council.

Saint Martin de Tours is the Patron Saint of Hospital Chaplains. A Roman centurion, he was known to tear up his cape and bandage the wounds of soldiers injured on the battlefield. Today roles of hospital chaplains can be specific such as rehabilitation, cardiac transplants, children, teamwork, permanent disabilities, surgery, palliative care, faith and identity, organ transplant, out-patients, terminal illness and ethical issues.

For many years the hospital chaplain was given the stereotype of simply swimming out to a drowning person, handing them a Bible as a path to salvation and then swimming safely back to shore! Or as Gerard W Hughes writes:

---

[55] Code of ethics for Catholic Social Services Australia 2006, 1.2 http://catholicsocialservices.org.au/system/files/Code_of_Ethics_06.pdf

I heard of an experiment on students studying for ministry, who were visiting a hospital. They were told they were to do a memory test. Someone would read them a story in one room. Then they were to proceed to another room, where they were to repeat the story as word perfectly as possible. The story read to them was a parable of the good Samaritan. In the corridor between rooms there was a patient lying in pain and crying for help. The patient was ignored by the single-minded students.[56]

This is no longer the accepted image and research is revealing the importance of the work of the chaplain from a scientific and economical mindset. Health care chaplaincy today seeks to improve the quality measures of its pastoral care services demonstrating its efficiency and effectiveness amid competing professionalism and funding.

Furthermore, training skills for pastoral care are now available through Australian Catholic University, Master of Ministry at the Sydney College of Divinity, Mental Health Care training needed in the Defence Force, Theological courses, Health Care chaplaincy courses, biomedical courses, and LaTrobe Pastoral Care and Palliative Courses.

Over 300 clinical staff from the Royal Children's Hospital (RCH) in Melbourne, including doctors, nurses and health professionals, identified several reasons why they valued having resident chaplains, including chaplaincy provides assistance with:

a. teamwork, including improving staff time management;

b. religious and psycho-social support to patients and staff through support in religious faith and connection with church communities;

c. specialist support to families and staff, particularly at times of death and grieving, and

---

[56] Gerard W Hughes, *Oh God Why? A spiritual journey towards meaning, wisdom and strength*, (Oxford: The Bible Reading Fellowship, 1996), 178.

d. provide input in terms of (i) ethical decision making, (ii) being a community link, (iii) providing a non-diagnostic communication role within the hospital and (iv) alleviating emotional discomfort for staff and patients within a complex and sometimes frightening institution.[57]

Hospital chaplains and pastoral carers may also in moments of crisis, have a special responsibility to sustain the physician. These occasions may range from frequently affirming the importance of the doctor's calling to wrestling over an ethical dilemma, assisting doctors in their constant confrontation with old age, disease, and death, or comforting the doctor whose patient has died.[58]

---

[57] Research conducted at the RCH Melbourne explored the role of chaplains which included nurses, doctors and all allied health professionals (Carey, Aroni, Edwards, 1997). The majority of clinical staff affirmed all the roles of hospital chaplains as being appropriate within a medical setting but emphasized that there needed to be extensions to the chaplains' role in terms: (i) increasing their public profile beyond the traditional stereotypes, (ii) assist staff with more productive teamwork, (iii) have a greater input on ethics committees and ethical decision making (iv) be more forthright in personal presentation and (v) increase chaplains to patient/staff ratio. An additional issue was the need for 'outpatient chaplaincy' and home visits enabling follow-up pastoral care. Both patients and staff value the various roles of chaplains within the hospital ie, sacramental, prayer, teamworker, educator, counsellor, witness role and when the chaplain ministers to the dying. Preliminary findings from the 'Liver Transplant and Pastoral Care' research, conducted within three Australian Hospitals, suggested that where chaplains are liaising and drawing patients, relatives and staff members together, the patients are more content and are being discharged at a faster rate (Elliot & Carey, 1996). The Westmead Brain Injury Rehabilitation Unit and Pastoral Care Department pilot research (Ireland, Carey, et al, 1999) which surveyed patients, relatives and visitors over a 12 month period indicated that 'irrespective of gender, age, category status, or religious belief the majority of respondents believed the chaplaincy services provided were 'very good' or 'good' (96.3%).'

[58] Evans, 'Healing in the Midst of Dying: A Collaborative Approach to End-of-Life Care,' 171.

It is desirable to incorporate the roles of chaplain or pastoral carer, the physician, and the nurse as co-equals and collaborators. Physicians start with the anatomical, physiological and diagnostic. Ministers begin with the need for reconciliation, the need to deal with guilt, the meaning of illness, and the person's spiritual destiny. The aim of both medicine and theology is to understand more clearly the reason for human suffering and to seek ways to relieve it. Abigail Evans writes, as medicine is called upon to sustain life, theology can assist in exploring the meaning of life as well as avenues for spiritual healing. When no cure is possible, ministers can reduce suffering, relieve anxiety, and offer inner peace.[59]

Chaplains may not be welcomed by a patient the first, second or even the third time, but driven by care, they keep coming back.

### Practical care

Sickness literature identifies three emotions generally present to some degree among hospitalised persons: anxiety, alienation and fear. These emotions may be related to a number of factors such as the suddenness of hospitalisation, the reason for admission, medical tests, procedures (chemotherapy, radiotherapy, surgical procedures, intensive care etc.), diagnosis and treatment, uncertain future, pain and discomfort of the illness, possibility of dying, care of and relationship with family, pets, work commitments, long-standing social obligations such as providing transport to school or work, sharing hospital accommodation with strangers, lack of privacy, loss of control and independence, visitors and meals, and the need to conform to expected behaviour of patients.[60] Disease, distress and the hospital environment may make people feel

---

[59] Evans, 'Healing in the Midst of Dying: A Collaborative Approach to End-of-Life Care,' 170.

[60] Frank Lopez, *Applied Pastoral Care: A Contextual Approach*, (Hunters Hill: Marist Centre for Pastoral Care, 1995), 100.

alienated and disconnected from their social and religious network, which would normally help one maintain a sense of identity and self respect.

The word 'pain' originates from the Greek word *poine*, which means penalty, and the Latin word *poena* meaning punishment. Galen, a famous Greek physician, made the first discovery that pain, associated with the sensation of touch, was related to the central nervous system and brain function, however it was Cicely Saunders who developed the concept of total pain that involves physical, mental, social and spiritual factors.[61] Factors influencing pain and pain perceptions include the disease, anxiety and other emotions, losses, difficulties in health system, communication and relationship, unique patient aspects, and side effects of treatment.[62]

Patients or families, often approach carers in regards to the over use or under use of drugs, in controlling pain. The pastoral carer may act as advocate, by bringing to attention of the nursing or medical staff, issues of concern such as inadequate pain management.[63] The Catholic Health Australia Code of Ethical Standards states:

> Health and aged care depends upon trusting collaboration between patients, residents, practitioners and carers. They thus require mutual respect, trust, honest communication and appropriate confidentiality. Patients and residents have the primary responsibility for judging which treatment and care options serve their authentic good in the totality of their circumstances. When people are incapable of making their own decisions, their family, guardian or other legal representative and the senior doctor (or other relevant professional) have the responsibility of

---

[61] Lindsay B. Carey, Christopher J. Newell and Bruce Rumbold, 'Pain Control and Chaplaincy in Australia' in *Journal of Pain and Symptom Management* 32, no. 6, (December 2006), 589-590.

[62] Arandra S, Buchanan J, Green G, Hodder P. 'The practice of palliative care. In *The creative option of palliative care*. Hodder P, Turley A., eds. (Melbourne: City Mission, 1989), 11-33.

[63] Carey, 'Pain Control and Chaplaincy in Australia' 599.

discerning what is in the patient's or resident's best interest, in the light of what is known of the patient's wishes.[64]

Aside from pain control, pastoral carers may be called to offer assistance to patients to interpret their pain experience. This emerges when concepts of pain, being caused by 'evil spirits' or punishment by a god, is the held belief. This can be addressed with the understanding of reconciliation, love, and forgiveness, in order to alleviate any guilt that may be affecting the person's healing. Various religious rituals may be used including reconciliation or blessings to assist patients in expressing and hopefully alleviating their pain.[65]

Illnesses caused by a single defective gene include muscular dystrophy, Cystic fibrosis, Down Syndrome, sickle cell anaemia and Huntington's disease. Autism, Alzheimer's, multiple sclerosis, and Parkinson's also seem to be genetically linked. Even diseases such as diabetes, heart disease and cancer, are frequently accompanied by genetic alterations. The technologies of genetic engineering, stem cell research, and cloning hold promises of therapies or cures. Yet for those with religious beliefs, such modern medical technologies may conflict with their religious values. Dilemmas may arise as to the possibility of accessing modern technology. Pastoral carers need to be sensitive to the person's decisions which arise out of circumstances of anguish and need for recovery.

Pastoral carers may also be called upon to facilitate possible dormant feelings of rage, frustration and doubt. To seek to rationalise the experience of sufferers may add to their agony. Rather patients seek permission by carers to lament and to question. There is the need to re-affirm integrity and attribute meaningful outcomes to physical or

---

[64] Catholic Health Australia. Code of Ethical Standards for catholic Health and Aged Care Services in Australia, 2001, no. 5.
http://www.stvincents.com.au/assets/files/pdf/CodeofEthicalStandards.pdf
[65] Carey, 'Pain Control and Chaplaincy in Australia,' 590.

emotional suffering.[66] Christian pastoral care is about holding the patients in empathy, restoring feelings of hope and peace, and searching for spiritual meaning and resolution.

Aside from advice on pain control and possibilities in accessing medical advancements, pastoral carers may be asked to pray for a miracle by the patient and their families. There are cases of miraculous recovery but these are few. So what do we say to those seeking a miracle? Thea Bowman writes, 'When I first found out I had cancer, I didn't know what to pray for. I didn't know if I should pray for healing or life or death. Then I found peace in praying for what my folks call 'God's perfect will.' As it evolved, my prayer has become, 'Lord, let me live until I die.' By that I mean I want to live, love, and serve fully until death comes. If that prayer is answered... how long really doesn't matter. Whether it's just a few months or a few years is really immaterial.'[67]

Holding out hope for a person's recovery can be a way of isolating oneself from them. Sometimes the person is ready to die but in many cases they want to be affirmed, encouraged and gently eased into the process of dying. Being the miracle is being the gentle and loving presence that offers inner peace to those who struggle, to be the light for those in darkness and hope for those struggling with despair. Preparing the person to accept their state with grace is the miracle.

At the same time pastoral carers may need to intervene when conversations between patient, their families, and the physicians become adversarial. This often arises because doctors speak from a biomedical

---

[66] Lawrence, Robert M., Julia Head, Georgina Christodoulou, Biljana Andonovska, Samina Karamat, Anita Duggal, Jonathan Hillam and Sarah Eagger. 'Spiritual advisors and old age psychiatry in the United Kingdom' in *Mental health, Religion and Culture* 11 (3), 2008.

[67] Therese J. Borchard, 'Let Me Live Until I Die: An Interview with Thea Bowman.' Accessed 3rd March 2012.
http://psychcentral.com/blog/archives/2010/10/17/let-me-live-until-i-die-an-interview-with-thea-bowman/

perspective and patients or families from a religious one. The patients may misunderstand the medico-moral teachings of their own religion. Here the pastoral care giver needs to help reinterpret the patient's theological understanding of the situation.

Pastoral care is more on restoring persons to well-being than on health. Patients need to cling to some assurance that they have a place and that life would not go on so smoothly if they simply disappeared. For patients, their prime task, if they cannot get over their sickness, is to try to regain their lost or diminished humanness in some other way. The patient's search for control may involve looking for meaning in their experience of illness, learning to communicate more effectively with health professionals, addressing personal and family issues, making arrangements for death, and participating as far as possible in decision-making which concerns their care. In regards to children who are sick the Code of Ethical Standards states:

> Children and babies have special needs when they are sick. Pain and other symptoms of illness can be overwhelming for young children who are unable fully to understand the causes of their distress, nor able to find meaning in their experience... A child naturally looks to his or her parents and family for support. As far as is practicable, Catholic healthcare services should provide facilities to enable the family to remain with a sick child.[68]

Hospital visitation has the intention of bringing hope, compassion and friendship to the other. What patients need is a listening ear, supportive words, forgiveness and companionship. Patients pray for their own health concerns, for wellness and about specific medical problems and expressed the desire that their physicians pray with them and that prayer be part of their spiritual and pastoral care.

---

[68] Code of Ethical Standards – Catholic Health Australia for Catholic Health and Aged Care Services in Australia, no. 4.19.
http://www.stvincents.com.au/assets/files/pdf/CodeofEthicalStandards.pdf

As ministers for Christ, praying with or for the sick person is a service to offer along with sharing the comfort of the words of Scripture. As persons are bed bound often in hospital for lengthy periods of time, the pastoral carer may become a link to the outside world. At the same time when one leaves the person's side, the pastoral carer can give practical help for the rest of the family through such initiatives as meals or babysitting. Once recovery begins, helping the person re-establish a sense of control and enjoyment of life is a way to offer care. So let us end this chapter with a Jewish story that awakens us to our greater responsibility to care:

> Once upon a time, a congregation became very concerned because their old rabbi had taken to disappearing from the synagogue after the opening of Shabbat. Some were afraid he was forgetting his proper duties. Some worried that he was actually breaking the Sabbath laws. Some, knowing his reputation for holiness, insisted that he must be being spirited up to heaven, perhaps even by Elijah himself, to discuss holy questions, to escape the problems of the age. So to settle the concerns among them, one Sabbath night they dispatched a spy to follow him and report where he was going. Sure enough, no sooner had the Sabbath candles been lit than the old man slipped out of the synagogue, walked quietly down the path, through the woods, and up a tall mountain. Finally, following quietly behind, the spy could see a small cabin in the distance. And sure enough, the rabbi went straight toward it. The spy crept closer. A few more steps and the spy could see the rabbi framed in the doorway by the soft light of a dying fire. The spy slipped around to the side of the cabin and pressed his face to the window. He could never have imagined the scene he saw. There on a cot lay an old gentile woman, her face sallow, her breathing slow. First, the rabbi swept the floor. Then the rabbi chopped new wood and fed the fire. Next the rabbi drew clean water from the well. Finally, the rabbi made a cauldron of fresh soup and set it on the bedstand by her side. The spy sped back down the mountain and through the woods to make his report: 'Well,' the congregation said, some with disdain, some with hope, 'did our rabbi go up to heaven?' The spy stopped for a moment to

think. 'No,' the spy said. 'The rabbi did not go up to heaven. The rabbi went much higher than that.'⁶⁹

---

⁶⁹ Joan D. Chittister, *Welcome to the wisdom of the world,* (Grand Rapids, Michigan: William B. Eerdmans, 2007), 100.

# Chapter 7: Pastoral care of the elderly

What Do You See, Nurse?
What do you see, nurse, what do you see? What are you thinking when you look at me? A crabbed old woman, not very wise, uncertain of habit with faraway eyes? Who dribbles her food and makes no reply? When you say in a loud voice, 'I do wish you'd try.' Who seems not to notice the things that you do and forever is losing a stocking or shoe? Who, resisting or not, lets you do as you will with bathing and feeding, the long day to fill? Is that what you're thinking, is that what you see? Then open your eyes; you're not looking at me. I'll tell you who I am as I sit here so still as I move at your bidding, as I eat at your will. I am a small child with a father and mother, brothers and sisters who love one another. A young girl of sixteen with wings at her feet, dreaming that soon now a lover she'll meet. A bride soon at twenty, my heart gives a leap, remembering the vows that I promised to keep. At twenty-five, now I have young of my own, who need me to build a secure, happy home. A woman of thirty, my young now grow fast, bound to each other with ties that should last. At forty, my young now soon will be gone, but my man stays beside me to see I don't mourn. At fifty, once more babies play around my knee. Again we know children, my loved one and me. Dark days are upon me, my husband is dead. I look at the future, I shudder with dread. For my young are all busy rearing young of their own and I think of the years and the love I have known. I'm an old lady now and nature is cruel, 'tis her jest to make old age look like a fool. The body it crumbles, grace and vigour depart and now there's a stone where I once had a heart. But inside this old carcass, a young girl still dwells and now and again my battered heart swells. I remember the joys, I remember the pain, and I am loving and living life over again. I think of the years all too few, gone so fast and accept the stark fact that nothing can last. Open your eyes, nurse, open and see not a crabbed old woman, look closer - see me.[70]

---

[70] Author unknown. Accessed 3rd March 2012. http://www.nursinghomealert.com/seeme.html

'My Father Began as a God' by Ian Mudie
My father began as a god, full of heroic tales of days when he was young. His ways were as immutable as if brought down from Sinai, which indeed he thought they were. He fearlessly lifted me to heaven by a mere swing to his shoulder and made of me a godling by seating me astride our milch-cow's back, and, too, upon a great white gobbler of which others went in constant fear. Strange then how he shrank and shrank until by my time of adolescence he had become a foolish small old man with silly and outmoded views of life and of morality. Stranger still that as I became older his faults and his intolerances scaled away into the past, revealing virtues such as honesty, generosity, integrity. Strangest of all how the deeper he recedes into the grave the more I see myself as just one more of all the little men who creep through life not knee-high to this long-dead god.[71]

## Australian Bureau of Statistics

By 2036, 6.3 million Australians will be aged 65 years or over, representing 24% of the nation's population.[72] There were 3.01 million people aged 65 years and over in Australia at June 2010, an increase of 370,600 people or 14.0% since June 2005. The proportion of people in this age group increased in each state and territory over this period, leading to an overall rise from 12.9% of the total population to 13.5%. The actual number of people aged 85 years and over is projected to more than quadruple within the next 40 years.

Very low infant and child mortality rates and high quality public and clinical health programs have seen Australia's life expectancy among the

---

[71] Ian Mudie, 'My Father Began as a God.' Accessed 3rd March 2012.
http://www.lakemac.infohunt.nsw.gov.au/library/links_level.asp?Level=2&LevelI D=151
[72] Australian Bureau of Statistics
http://www.agedcare.org.au/PUBLICATIONS-&-RESOURCES/General-pdfs-images/ACSA%20Fact%20Sheet%201%202008-%20An%20Ageing%20Australia.pdf

highest in the world. Yet along with Japan, Germany, New Zealand and Canada, it will experience a doubling in the proportion of the population aged 65 and over in the next 50 years.

The 2006 census also reveals just over 15,000 Indigenous Australians are aged 65 years and over. These figures indicate the Indigenous life expectancy rate is 17 years less than general Australian life expectancy rates, a National shame, which calls for immediate attention.

Australian Bureau of Statistics also reveals that more people aged 65 years and over are staying on at work. In 2007, there were five people of working age to support every person aged 65 and over. By 2047, there will be only 2.4 people of working age to support each person aged 65 and over. So what are the consequences of this?

With the projected increase of the population aged over 65, older people must be empowered to make diverse and important contributions to community. In economic terms, an ageing population creates both demand for services and potential economic stimuli. Yet an ageing Australia also requires that governments ensure services for older Australians are available, are of high quality and meet the needs of older people into the future.

## Age categories

Age categories for the elderly include: the young-old (65-75); the old (75-85 years old); and the old-old (85 and beyond). Gerontological research shows most old people continue earlier patterns of thought, emotion, behaviour, spirituality and religion of midlife, although physical and mental disabilities may precipitate.[73] With the passing of years, physical and social changes may undermine one's sense of security and wellbeing. Yet for many, aging is often a positive experience, and with coping skills acquired over time, one is able to generally function with effectiveness.

---

[73] Gollnick, *Religion and Spirituality in the Life Cycle*, 211.

Physical changes expected as one ages include lack of peak performance, decreases and losses are experienced such as hearing and sight, require advancement in medical treatment and specialised exercise programs etc. In psychological effects of the ageing person, mental abilities and personalities remain stable however roles, relationships, social and occupational status change. Retirement, relocation, death of spouse and close friends, and increase in chronic illnesses all challenge one to adapt. Spiritual changes arise through grieving, adjusting, compensating and rebuilding through the experiences the sadness and sorrows of life. Yet the experience of God's presence and love provides a sense of trust and hope.[74]

Erik Erikson characterizes the final stage of life as ego-integrity versus despair and disgust. The main achievement in this process is to accept one's life as something that had to be, even with its limitations and failures. If the elderly person is unable to reach a degree of emotional integration, despair develops with the realisation that time and energy no longer remain for building something that seems 'right.' Coming to terms with failures and missed opportunities as well as accomplishments, requires the elderly to experience a wide range of positive and negative emotions on their way to ego integrity.[75]

Full self actualisation is realised in self-transcendence where one moves beyond achievement and production, to search for something more. Combined active participation and reflective withdrawal allow for fulfilling experiences.

---

[74] Melvin A Kimble, 'Pastoral Care of the Elderly' in *The Journal of Pastoral Care*. Vol XLI, No. 3, September 1987:272.
[75] Gollnick, *Religion and Spirituality in the Life Cycle*, 219-220.

## The dignity of the elderly

In the Letter of Pope John Paul II to the elderly, in 1999, he offered thanks for his life and revisits his past, where struggles are now seen as opportunities to experience God's grace:

> I do so first of all by thanking God for the gifts and the opportunities which he has abundantly bestowed upon me up to now. In my memory I recall the stages of my life, which is bound up with the history of much of this century, and I see before me the faces of countless people, some particularly dear to me: they remind me of ordinary and extraordinary events, of happy times and of situations touched by suffering. Above all else, though, I see outstretched the provident and merciful hand of God the Father.[76]

The Pope emphasised the importance of Scripture which understands old age as a blessing and the elderly as full of wisdom. He then discussed the importance of the elderly in today's society:

> Elderly people help us to see human affairs with greater wisdom, because life's vicissitudes have brought them knowledge and maturity. They are the guardians of our collective memory, and thus the privileged interpreters of that body of ideals and common values which support and guide life in society. To exclude the elderly is in a sense to deny the past, in which the present is firmly rooted, in the name of a modernity without memory.[77]

According to the late Pope, the elderly continue to have a role to play in society including culture bearers and culture creators, evangelization of grandchildren, offering loving advice and guidance, silent prayers, and their witness of suffering borne with patient acceptance. However the elderly also need care and 'Everything becomes easier when each elderly

---

[76] Pope John Paul II Letter to the elderly, in 1999, paragraph 1. http://www.vatican.va/holy_father/john_paul_ii/letters/documents/hf_jp-ii_let_01101999_elderly_en.html

[77] Letter of his Holiness Pope John Paul II to the elderly, 1999, paragraph 10.

resident is helped by family, friends and parish communities to feel loved and still useful to society.'[78]

Due to their limited life expectancy, the elderly focus on what matters to them, their relationships, marriage, children and grandchildren. They frequently feel that they contribute to their grandchildren's development and take pride. Conversely, this connection to younger generations gives the elderly coherence. The following captures the wisdom reflected in the Pope's Letter. Titled 'Beatitudes for Friends of the Aged' it was written by Esther Mary Walker:[79]

> Blessed are they who seem to know that my eyes are dim and my wits are slow.
> Blessed are they who looked away when coffee spilled at table today.
> Blessed are they with a cheery smile who stop to chat for a little while.
> Blessed are they who never say, "You've told that story twice today."
> Blessed are they who know the way to bring back memories of yesterdays.
> Blessed are they who make it known that I'm loved, respected and not alone.
> Blessed are they who know I'm at a loss to find the strength to carry the Cross.
> Blessed are they who ease the days on my journey home in loving ways.

## Practical care

Features of the world of the elderly may include more free time, fewer needs, acquiring practical wisdom, surrounded by their children and grandchildren, coped with significant loss and death of family and friends, widowhood, decline in health, hearing and seeing abilities, wonder about the meaning of life, memory weakens, fears of decline in intellectual ability, loss of social status as productive workers, need to

---

[78] Letter of his Holiness Pope John Paul II to the elderly, 1999, paragraph 13.
[79] Esther Mary Walker, *Beatitudes for Friends of the Aged*, Year unknown. http://www.theexaminer.org/volume7/number2/aged.htm

achieve within the limiting constraints of ageing, need to address their spiritual needs, vulnerable to assault and robbery, declining finances, selling their homes and moving into a nursing home, becoming disabled and dependent on others, living in boredom, depression and fear, lonely and abandoned, a burden to their children, lack strength and energy, homebound, incontinent and the need to be fed, washed and dressed. Death is the ultimate challenge and paramount fear of many elderly.

In the movie Shawshank Redemption, the librarian Brooks has spent most of his life behind bars in a top security prison. Upon his unexpected release he finds himself alone in a world he has become unfamiliar with. Given a job bagging groceries and a small room to live in, he quickly spirals into depression, finding himself alone and frightened. As the scenario unfolds the elderly Brooks decides death is better than a life alone. Watching this poignant scene, one is confronted with the question, 'Do we really care about our aged neighbours who struggle to comprehend this ever changing, fast paced world?'

The disengagement theory argues that older people develop different values than the young, leading them to become less emotionally involved in the activities and social relationships that occupied them in mid life. Physical helplessness, loss of spouse, family and friends, and feelings of rejection, can undermine the ability and desire to remain active, with the vast majority of older people not taking advantage of available social opportunities such as senior centres.[80] They disengage from their social roles as their place in society and their health, diminish. Society reinforces this withdrawal through its lack of interest in, and opportunities for the elderly, but essentially disengagement is seen as a natural rather than an imposed process. The elderly should have time to reflect on their long experience and attend to their inner lives after years of conforming to occupational and social roles.[81]

---

[80] Gollnick, *Religion and Spirituality in the Life Cycle*, 207.
[81] Gollnick, *Religion and Spirituality in the Life Cycle*, 211.

Yet old age can also be a blessed time. Some get involved in lots of new interests and others feel finally free from duties, journeying towards communion and rediscovering the beauty and simplicity of daily life. This activity theory suggests that the more active older people are, the better mentally, physically and socially adjusted they become. New research suggests one of the most important contributors to successful ageing may be the extent to which we stay involved and active in our communities.

An old man and his wife entered a McDonald's store and ordered a cheeseburger meal. They sat down, cut the burger in half and the old man began to eat. The onlookers looked with pity on the poor couple. Eventually a young man got up, approached them and offered to buy them another meal. The old man replied that they shared everything. Still he ate while the old woman looked on. Again the young man offered to buy another meal for them. This time the old woman explained that they shared everything. The young man commented that if they shared everything, then why wasn't she eating her half of the cheeseburger? The old woman replied, 'I am waiting for the teeth!' It is a humorous story, but the love of an elderly couple sharing their trials together has a redemptive quality in which nothing hinders their journey of life together.

On Australian free to air television, the ABC Compass programme aired a documentary on the lives of three elderly people.[82] What emerges from all three interviews is the necessity for the elderly to continue to be part of a community, be it in the workplace or family life. As the interviewee Caroline Moses said, 'It's important to me to be part of community but not necessarily in a workplace. I think everybody has to have that sense of community somewhere, and I find I can get it from other things, like volunteering or being involved in other activities.' This finds support with theologian Thomas H. Groome's writing:

---

[82] Kim Akhurst, Story producer; Story researcher: Jeannine Baker. 'Work, Later On' *Compass programme*, 19 September 2010.

Our partnership with one another actualizes our partnership with God. I emphasize that the human condition is realized as a community-of-persons. We are ever person-in-community. Our human identity is first and foremost relational; we become who we are through relationship with other people. It is not that we become a person first and then relate; rather we become persons only by relating.[83]

Secondly all three elderly interviewees affirmed the usefulness of older persons in society and their essential contributions to the wider community. Peter Leith said, 'I'm not paid a great hourly rate but that's not relevant at all. I get such a lot from the people I meet and talk to Monday to Friday every week.' Caroline Moses also supported this by saying, 'I think as I get older the philosophy that guides me is purely I want to live life to the fullest, not in a kind of totally pleasurable sense. But in helping others, in keeping active, in just doing the right thing by other people. . . My husband and I mind two of our grandchildren every Thursday, and we both love it.' Mia the third interviewee said, 'Being a fitness instructor for seniors involves, at least from my perspective that you have to empathise with people's personal life. They come to the pool for various reasons. They have aches and pains and knees that don't work well and hips that ache and they sometimes have a lack of social contact so the pool becomes also something more than just exercises.'

The elderly need ways to interact with society for their self esteem and sense of purpose. Such ways include encouraging choice and decision-making or giving the elderly something new to do and have responsibility for such as a pot plant or garden patch. By encouraging the elderly and the dying to use their gifts for ministry in the church, the church imparts value to these later years and helps the aging to maintain a vital connection to the community.

There is a sense of urgency for the elderly to share their life story. The fear of forgetting and the need to remember both mark the last stage

---

[83] Groome, *What makes us Catholic. Eight gifts for life*, 60.

of their life. Life review helps older adults tell their story, who they are and where they have been.[84]

> Miss Manners... the truth is the most complex concept of all. It means getting to the truth of the situation, rather than the crude literal surface truth. To answer the question, 'Would you like to see some pictures of my grandchildren?' with the direct literal truth, 'No! Anything but that!' would be cruel. But is that the real question? The real question, if one has any sensitivity to humanity is, 'Would you be kind enough to let me share some of my sentiments and reassure me that they are important and worthwhile?' to which a decent person can only answer, 'I'd love to.'[85]

Care of the elderly deals with practical issues of ageing such as carers and financial assistance, homecare, palliative care, nursing home options, meals on wheels, day care centres, hostels, retirement village living, Medicare and age pensions, managing health, hospital services, complementary therapies (include chiropractic, osteopathy, naturopathy, acupuncture, acupressure and herbal medicines), personal security, making a will, donating organs, financial planning, government assistance, planning the funeral and coping with grief. Furthermore studies found that most elderly are diagnosed as having a disease three years before it will eventually end their lives. Chronic illness means that dying takes a longer period of time and involves more complicated medical issues. A slow death offers opportunities to spend time with family, say goodbye and slowly orient a person toward life with God. Major personal goals among the ageing according to Frank Lopez, include:[86]

1. Independence – the ability to provide for their own needs as an important goal.

---

[84] Kimble, 'Pastoral Care of the Elderly,' 275.
[85] Cleveland Plain Dealer, 21 June 1984, p5.
[86] Lopez, *Applied Pastoral Care: A Contextual Approach*, 109-110.

2. Social acceptability – to be seen as friendly and easy to get along with.
3. Conserving personal resources – to live without overstretching their personal energy sources.
4. Ability and strength to cope with adversity.
5. Ability to cope with personal change – with some improvement over their past selves.
6. Search for meaning in later life – the opportunity to relax more than in the past.

Respect for the dignity of older persons and solidarity with them requires care which fosters their opportunities to participate in family, church and community life and, if possible, to live in their home environment. In coping with loneliness, developing a relationship with God becomes an important factor. Pastoral support is of crucial importance in the context of aged care and should be geared around pastoral visits, counselling, group prayer, and opportunities for celebrating the sacraments and other religious rites.

## Aged care facilities

In the Australian Code of Ethical Standards it states, 'Every effort should be made to ensure that institutional environments for older persons respect their individuality and are as homelike as possible. In addition to high quality nursing care and social services as required, special provision should be made for the spiritual needs of older persons.'[87]

Aged care facilities assist the aged with residential and respite care services and to ensure they live a dignified, secure and rewarding life. The

---

[87] Code of Ethical Standards –Catholic Health Australia for Catholic Health and Aged Care Services in Australia. 4.4.
http://www.stvincents.com.au/assets/files/pdf/CodeofEthicalStandards.pdf

vision is based on the ideal to strengthen and promote the overall health and well-being of the individual created in the image and likeness of God. The values and mission of aged care facilities are founded on qualities such as love of Christ, compassion, justice and hope. Specific challenges which such Organisations have identified for the people they serve include:

- A number of residents may not have family members to support their hope that they belong, leading to emotional pain.
- Due to the age of the clients, some may ignore their abilities and capacities to look forward to life. With lack of motivation, confidence and self-esteem, they may refuse to participate in the activities provided for them.
- Inability to walk or eat, see or hear is difficult to accept at this stage of life.

Initiatives such organisations undertake to help the elderly maintain or recover a sense of hope may include:

- Maintaining an optimum standard of nursing care and high quality service.
- To acknowledge and uphold the dignity of each resident. To this end, healthcare should be given with compassion, care, love and encouragement with every consideration for privacy and comfort.
- To respect and protect the resident's rights and ensure their spiritual, physical and emotional needs are met, enabling them to live in peace and without pain.
- Offer comfortable, secure, pleasant, clean, well-aired and bright surroundings and create an atmosphere of homeliness.

- Notify the residents about their right to exercise freedom of choice and make their own decisions about personal aspects of daily life, financial affairs and possessions.
- Individuality of the residents to be emphasised and respected both in the care planning and in the way staff perform their duties.
- To develop confidence, self-esteem and competence for self-improvement. Activities can be arranged such as excursions to local events, trips, games, discussion groups, exercise groups, and BBQ's. Cooperation and support from relatives, friends, management and staff are encouraged.

This ministry must be done with great mercy and care. It follows that staff must see themselves and the patients as forming the equivalent of a family system. Staff should encourage residents to work towards maintaining an open environment where they are able to discuss their hopes, fears, frustrations, anger, joys, sorrows etc. However what happens when aged residents are from an ethnic background?

In 2006 people aged 65 and over from diverse linguistic and cultural backgrounds comprised one in three older Australians. The proportion born overseas at the 2006 census were 34% for those now aged 65-74 years, 30% for those aged 75-84 years, and 26% for those aged 85 years and over. So the question arises how best to serve the spiritual and pastoral needs of elderly people of ethnic background?

Aged care residencies may have a higher number of residents from a particular culture. Let us take for example The Maronite Sisters of the Holy Family Aged Care Facility which opened in 1998 in Sydney, and has a high number of residents from a Middle Eastern background. As the Sisters can speak Arabic, and organise for priests to preside over a Maronite Mass, as well as offering Lebanese cuisine and spiritual direction, many of the residents take great heart in this. They feel comfortable talking with Sisters who can understand them and their cultural and spiritual needs. Masses are also said for the Latin Rite residents as well as those who are Orthodox or Coptic.

When the elderly are respected and afforded opportunity to feel useful, loved and special and have their particular spiritual, cultural and linguistic needs met, they can enjoy their final years. So let us end this reflection of care for the elderly in our society with the prayer of a seventeenth century nun, which speaks of the frustrations, yet also the memories, dreams and hopes of the elderly.

> Lord, you know better than I know myself, that I am growing older and will someday be old. Keep me from the fatal habit of thinking I must say something on every subject and on every occasion. Release me from craving to straighten out everybody's affairs. Make me thoughtful but not moody; helpful but not bossy. With my vast store of wisdom, it seems a pity not to use it all, but you know, Lord, that I want a few friends at the end. Keep my mind free from the recital of endless details; give me the wings to get to the point. Seal my lips on my aches and pains. They are increasing, and love of rehearsing them is becoming sweeter as the years go by. I dare not ask for grace enough to enjoy the tales of others' pains, but help me to endure them with patience. I dare not ask for improved memory, but for a growing humility, and a lessening cocksureness when my memory seems to clash with the memory of others. Teach me the glorious lesson that occasionally I may be mistaken. Keep me reasonably sweet. I do not want to be a saint (some of them are so hard to live with) but a sour old person is one of the crowning works of the devil. Give me the ability to see good things in unexpected places and talents in unexpected people. And give me, O Lord, the grace to tell them so.[88]

---

[88] Wisdom from the 17th century: an anonymous nun's prayer, *AD2000* Vol 17 No 2 (March 2004), p. 13
http://www.ad2000.com.au/articles/2004/mar2004p13_1562.html

## Chapter 8: Pastoral care of the dying

We have begun to realize, I believe, that the enemy all along was not death, but our own unwillingness to incorporate its reality into our consciousness - **Sandol Stoddard**[89]

I die every day - **1 Cor 15:31**

Death and life are not simply two events which follow one upon another and are distinct one from the other in human existence. They interpenetrate one another. We are in process of dying all through our lives, and what we call death is the culminating point of an act of dying that extends over the whole span of life. That is why we are constantly undergoing a foretaste of that descent into death which the Lord took upon himself. Do we not sometimes feel an immeasurable distance lay silently between us and the things of this world, dividing us from them? Are we not slowly in process of becoming those who depart? Are we not constantly and ever anew saying goodbye? Is not that which is familiar to us changing to an ever-increasing extent into that which is alien and almost hostile and repellent? Long before the hour in which we close our eyes for the last time we are already being drawn back into the depths of their world. This descent into the poverty of our own being has already commenced, and has been in progress ever since we received our human natures, even though only in an invisible and hidden manner, at the roots of our being - **Karl Rahner**[90]

## Belief in life after death

Eastern religions such as Hinduism and Buddhism believe in reincarnation and the final attainment of nirvana. The concept of a heaven or paradise where one shares eternal life with God after death was

---

[89] Sandol Stoddard, *The Hospice Movement*, (New York: Vintage Books, 1992), 8.
[90] Karl Rahner, *Theological Investigations,* Vol. VII, (Herder and Herder), 149-150.

taken up by the Semitic religions including Judaism, Christianity and Islam. This human instinct for something beyond death can be traced back to even earlier centuries where Palaeolithic burial sites (50,000 BCE) were found to contain food, weapons, ornaments, and tools, suggesting people believed even back then that the dead would somehow come to exist again. In tribal life there is the strong sense of identity with one's people, and so there is less protest of death. The natural process of birth and death are observed in nature and celebrated in tribal ritual.

Physical life and death are complimentary to each other, rather than opposites. With a transcendent view of life, it enables people to place their lives and suffering in a larger, meaningful context. Death then becomes the moment when a person brings their existence to a meaningful conclusion.

For Christians, hope in life after death is based on the Resurrection of Jesus, proclaimed in the Gospels and Letters. Christ says, 'I am with you always' (Mt 28:20). The Cross is a symbol of the victory of life over death and Christ enables each one of us to make a passing over from death to life. It is the deep Christian truth that, 'unless a wheat grain falls into the ground and dies, it remains only a single grain; but if it dies it yields a rich harvest' (Jn 12:24).

In Rm 6:3-5 we read, 'Do you not know that all of us who have been baptized into Christ Jesus were baptised into his death? Therefore we have been buried with him by baptism into death, so that, just as Christ was raised from the dead by the glory of the Father, so we too might walk in newness of life.' Baptised into Christ we believe we share his life, although we do not know what our life will mean beyond the grave.

For Paul, Christ's resurrection was only the beginning of God's plan, which leads to the defeat of evil forces and the resurrection of all Christ's faithful on the final day, 'Listen, I will tell you a mystery! We will not all die, but we will all be changed, in a moment, in the twinkling of an eye, at the last trumpet. For the trumpet will sound, and the dead will be raised imperishable, and we will be changed. For this perishable body must put on imperishability, and this mortal body must put on immortality' (1 Cor 15:51-53). God raised Jesus to life and thereby made him the bringer of life to all. By calling Christ the first fruits, resurrection of the believing dead is inevitable.

## Stages of death

Henri Nouwen relates a story:

> Recently a student who had just finished his long studies for the ministry and was ready to start in his first church suddenly died after a fatal fall from his bike. Those who knew him well felt a strong, angry protest arising from their hearts. Why him, a very noble man who could have done so much for so many? Why now, just when his long, costly education could start bearing fruit? Why in this way, so unprepared and unheroic? There were no answers to all these reasonable questions. A strong angry protest seemed the only human response.[91]

These deaths oblige people to face their own death as they realise, 'This could have been me.' Death is a daily process physiologically, psychologically and spiritually. According to Stephen R. Covey, we must ask what is the meaning of our lives, in order to live it fully up to the moment of death. In order to do this, he provides an exercise which is adapted here.[92]

You are invited to sit down, collect your thoughts and focus on what you are about to do. Think of three people you know well: a family member, friend and workmate. Now imagine yourself sitting at the back of a long Church while everyone you know is sitting in front of you. Suddenly you realize you are watching your own funeral, years from now. The three people you have chosen will be doing your obituary. What would you like each one to say about you and your life? How do you want

---

[91] Henri J. M. Nouwen, *Reaching Out. The three movements of the Spiritual Life*, (New York: Image Books Double day, 1986), 131.
[92] Stephen R. Covey, *The 7 habits of highly effective people*, 2004.

them to remember you? Covey suggests you take some time to reflect and then begin to write down the three eulogies. This exercise, when done attentively, awakens one to the limitedness of our days but also its potential possibilities.

The five stages of grieving/dying formulated by Dr Elizabeth Kubler-Ross in her 1969 book, *On Death and Dying* include:[93]

> Stage 1: Denial - This is not happening to me. Denial gives people time until they are ready to tackle with the necessary changes.
> Stage 2: Anger - How dare God do this to me. The basis of this anger is a result of feeling loss of control in one's life.
> Stage 3: Bargaining - Just let me live to see my daughter marry. By buying time one hopes to gain control.
> Stage 4: Depression - I can't bear to face going through this, putting my family through this. The person experiences sadness but tries to come to terms with the anticipated loss.
> Stage 5: Acceptance - I'm ready, I don't want to struggle anymore. When the reality of death is accepted as part of being human, one becomes ready to die. Elderly people generally move to this acceptance largely on their own, while others may need assistance.

Since Kubler-Ross' formulation, there have been other stages developed. Wayne Oates suggested grief is expressed in six stages: 1. Shocking blow of loss-in-itself 2. Numbing effect of the shock 3. Struggle between fantasy and reality 4. Break-through of a flood of grief 5. Selective memory and stabbing pain. 6. And acceptance of loss and reaffirmation of life itself.[94]

David Switzer recognised four common phases of grief: 1. Feeling of numbness and denial 2. Yearning for and preoccupation with thoughts of

---

[93] Dr Elizabeth Kubler-Ross, *On Death and Dying*, 1969.
[94] Steven L. Jeffers and Harold Ivan Smith, *Finding a sacred oasis in grief. A resource manual for pastoral caregivers*, (Oxford: Radcliffe Publishing, 2007), 85.

the deceased person 3. Disorganisation and despair and 4. Reorganization of behaviour.[95]

There are other theories of grief. However there has been criticism of the stages as individuals experience grief uniquely and each person needs their own time to reflect and grapple with the mystery of death, for the grief to be eventually reconciled. Yet the stages do recognise important emotions that pastoral carers need to be aware of.

**Palliative and hospice care**

Hope in medicine can lead to an unrealistic expectation that medicine can cure whatever disease one might have. Yet Christian doctors, ethicists, pastors and theologians believe that while aggressive care has its place, there must come a point when Christians shift their focus from extending life to preparing to die. The following scenario by Kohlberg, paints in stark image one's quest for human survival:

> In Europe, a woman was near death from a special kind of cancer. There was one drug that the doctors thought might save her. It was a form of radium that a druggist in the same town had recently discovered. The drug was expensive to make, but the druggist was charging ten times what the drug cost him to make. He paid $200 for the radium and charged $2,000 for a small dose of the drug. The sick woman's husband, Heinz, went to everyone he knew to borrow the money, but he could only get together about $1,000 which is half of what it cost. He told the druggist that his wife was dying and asked him to sell it cheaper or let him pay later. But the druggist said, 'No, I discovered the drug and I'm going to make money from it.' So Heinz got desperate and broke into the man's store to steal the drug for his wife.[96]

There comes a time when doctors, families and patients need to know when to forgo medical treatment intended to cure and turn instead to

---

[95] Jeffers and Smith, *Finding a sacred oasis in grief. A resource manual for pastoral caregivers*, 86.
[96] Lawrence Kohlberg, *Stages of Moral Development*, 1963, p. 19

treatment that promotes comfort.[97] The Australian Code of Ethical Standards states:

> In receiving physical, psychological, social and spiritual support, patients may need help to make the most of what remains of their lives, not only by the alleviation of their suffering but also by the respect accorded their personal dignity and the quality of their living. Vulnerable patients may need to be protected from pressures which lower their self-esteem or encourage self-abandonment. They may need help not only with the many symptoms of illness such as pain and discomfort and its psychological sequelae such as anxiety, fear and distress, but also with its spiritual effects such as crises of faith, hope and love.[98]

In the concern to ensure patients who are terminally ill are treated with utmost respect, hospices and palliative care have been established.

The Latin word, *hospice*, means both host and guest. It is holistic care, where a team of physicians, nurses, health aides, social workers, chaplains, bereavement counsellors, and volunteers all minister to the physical, emotional and spiritual well-being of the terminally ill person and their family. Hospice tries to establish a setting that gives the terminally ill dignity, privacy, love, care, support and some control over the remainder of their lives. Hospice care can be delivered in private homes, nursing homes and in some hospitals, where patients reside until they die.[99] In Singapore, hospices are fitted with ponds, fish and greenery, which offer a sense of inner peace and calm.

Similar to hospice care, palliative care is oriented to caring for, and accompanying a dying person in the final phase of life, while upholding the person's dignity and respecting their spiritual, physical, emotional

---

[97] Rob Moll, *The Art of Dying*, (Downers Grove, Illinois: IVP Books, 2010), 109.
[98] Code of Ethical Standards, 5.5.
[99] Glavan, 'Death and dying,' 9.

and social needs. It also encompasses care for bereaved family and friends.

Although there are deaths that are unexpected, violent or tragic, many more people await death in hospitals and homes, over days and possibly over years. Through pastoral care and hospice and palliative care, the intention is for a gentle and peaceful death, where people do not die alone but surrounded with kin and much love.

## Practical care

In the recent Japanese film *Departures. The gift of last memories*, it sensitively tells the story of a young man who at first reluctantly takes up the job of preparing human corpses for burial. The job becomes ironically life giving for the young man and those grieving. The realisation dawns that relationships and memories of the deceased are paramount as is the desire to offer the greatest care and dignity during the final moments.

As people enter into a battle with God, search for meaning in their lives and in their illnesses, they begin to grieve while grappling with their faith. Pastoral carers need to be available early in an illness to build up trust and create an atmosphere of compassionate listening and gently lead one to gradually redefine and rediscover hope and peace for themselves.

A facet of pastoral companionship is to facilitate direct expression of memories, feelings, worries and tensions. They set the stage for a more sustaining mutual support as the illness progresses. The assembly of supportive friends and family around the dying serves to remind the patient of their meaningful relationships.

Having end-of-life conversations, making wise choices toward a good death and being present with dying loved ones are important. Patients seek warm relationships, to be listened to, have someone to share their fears and concerns with, have someone around to pray with, and to have a chance to say goodbye to loved ones. They want to believe and be assured they will be in the presence of a loving God at the moment of death. Sister Dolores one of the Missionaries of Charity founded by Blessed Mother Teresa states:

> It's quite simple really. The dying are moved by the love they receive and it may be just a touch of my hand, or a glass of water, or providing them with some kind of sweet they desire. You just take that to them, what they ask for, and they are satisfied and know someone cares for them, someone loves them, someone wants them – and that, in itself, is a great help to them. Because of this they believe that God must be even kinder and more generous and so their souls are lifted up to God. As we don't preach and just do what we do with love, they are touched by God's grace.[100]

Throughout history, Christians have sought to die well. Such a death includes expressing willingness to die, the opportunity for last words and final thoughts and encouragements to family and friends. The days before death should be a time of reconciliation with estranged family and friends and possibly even with God, a time to communicate forgiveness and a release from hurts inflicted in the past. It is a time for listening and being present and placing the loved one in the hands of Christ. The approach of death can also be a time of thanksgiving and hope for all of God's gifts during one's earthly life. Prayer, Bible reading, religious service and other spiritual disciplines prepare a person's transitioning to life in eternity, while also being a source of spiritual strength for a congregation and the family.

During the last days before death, pastoral care frequently takes the form of gently urging the family to let go and allow their loved one to die. In the final hours words become far less important than simple gestures and a shared silence. No longer pre-occupied with reviewing their lives nor focused on the concerns of those around them, critically ill persons begin to say good-bye. Since close loved ones can become offended by a dying person's turning inward and can feel agitated as verbal

---

[100] Lucinda Vardey (ed.), *Mother Teresa. A Simple path*, (Sydney: Rider, 1995), 90.

communication becomes less and less, pastoral ministers have to reassure relatives and friends that silence does not mean rejection.[101]

Sitting with a family, encouraging them to hold the hand of a loved one or to put a cold cloth on the perspiring forehead or to moisten parched lips with a little water, offering prayer, signing the cross on the forehead, bringing coffee for family members, supporting them in touching the body and talking to it, protecting their privacy as each close relative says goodbye alone, putting an arm around a bereaved member, crying with them. At death simple prayer brings closure and gives the family an invitation to separate themselves from the place of death.[102]

Victor E Frankl tells of a young woman who knew that she would die in the next few days. 'I am grateful that fate has hit me so hard,' she told me. 'In my former life, I was spoiled and did not take spiritual accomplishments seriously.' Pointing through the window of the hut, she said, 'This tree here is the only friend I have in my loneliness.' Through that window, she could see just one branch of a chestnut tree, and on the branch were two blossoms. 'I often talk to this tree,' she said to me. I was startled and didn't quite know how to take her words. Was she delirious? Did she have occasional hallucinations? Anxiously I asked her if the tree replied. 'Yes.' What did it say to her? She answered, "It said to me, 'I am here - I am here - I am life, eternal life.'"[103]

The process of dying is a basic physical event that is surrounded with mystery and miracle. People have described feeling a spiritual presence at someone's death, as if the person who died were still there. Still others tell of loved ones talking to already deceased family members as they neared death, as if dead loved ones had come to assist in the journey. It is a reminder that within the Christian tradition is an experience of ongoing,

---

[101] Gerald J. Calhoun, *Pastoral Companionship. Ministry with seriously-ill persons and their families*, (New York: Paulist Press, 1986), 106.
[102] Calhoun, *Pastoral Companionship. Ministry with seriously-ill persons and their families*, 107.
[103] Frankl, *Man's search for Meaning*, 69.

communal presence. Through rites and practices, the church maintains a constant and unbroken presence to those who are dying beyond the point of their burial.

## The ethical issue of life support

The Australian Code of Ethical Standards states:

> In current Australian medical practice and legislation, a person is said to be dead when there is either irreversible cessation of the circulation of the blood or irreversible cessation of all function of the brain (so called 'brain death'). Generally death is determined by the irreversible loss of cardio-respiratory function. However, modern medical technology often severs the links between death and the cessation of cardio-respiratory function. It has thus become necessary to recognise that in the absence of all brain function it is impossible for a person to live as an integrated and coordinated organism. Total and irreversible loss of all brain function, accompanied by an evident cause, is thus a valid medical criterion of death.[104]

It continues, 'Pressures to change the way death is determined from the loss of *all* brain function to the loss of *some* brain function should be resisted. Rather, Catholic hospitals should lead the way in trying to perfect the diagnostic criteria for death.'[105]

An issue that may arise in caring for the terminally ill is the possibility of euthanasia either when a patient seeks no longer to continue life, to comply with the wishes of the family, to assist suicide, or to vacate a bed. Suicide and euthanasia are stark examples of death resistance. Euthanasia is any action (such as administering deliberate overdoses of otherwise appropriate medications), or omission (such as unjustified withholding or

---

[104] Code of Ethical Standards in regards to *Clinical markers of death*, 5.22
[105] Code of Ethical Standards, 5.23.

withdrawing life sustaining forms of care) which of itself and by intention causes death with the purpose of eliminating all suffering.[106]

The withdrawal of life support technology is one of the most difficult decisions faced by doctors, patients and their families. Most wish for their loved ones a peaceful and dignified death, yet many worry that their decision to terminate life support might make them instrumental in that death. From a Catholic perspective it is never permissible to end a person's life.

Medical professionals use four criteria to determine the legitimacy of discontinuing mechanical life support.

1. The presence of a fatal condition - If the patient stands a good chance of recovery, life support should by all means be used (which is most cases such as those recovering from surgery, premature infants, recovering from trauma).
2. The autonomy of the patient - If the patient is conscious, able to communicate, and capable of rational decision making, their desires are paramount. They have every right to refuse a particular medical treatment.
3. Whether the therapy is effective - If there is no medical benefit it is stopped. Doctors may withhold or discontinue treatments that are deemed to be futile, ie the patient suffers a terminal condition, the condition is irreversible, and that death is imminent.
4. If a given medical treatment places an excessive burden on the patient, family or community.[107]

---

[106] Code of Ethical Standards , 5.20.
[107] Noreen Herzfeld, *Technology and Religion. Remaining human in a co-created world,* (West Conshohocken, PA: Templeton Press, 2009), 50-52.

Discontinuing life support is not euthanasia because it does not introduce a new cause of death according to ethicists. Morally speaking, the intention is not to cause death but to ease the physical or psychological burden on either the patient or the patient's family. The questions about what one should do concerning cardiopulmonary resuscitation (CPR), ventilator support, feeding tubes, intravenous lines (IVs) antibiotics and other interventions to provide life support, requires moral advice by the pastoral carer.

From a religious perspective Christians are expected to use all ordinary means to care for the sick and help the suffering. The Catholic Church has a 500 year tradition of permitting patients and their families to forgo extraordinary care. The permanent need for life sustaining machinery, such as a ventilator or dialysis machine, in the face of terminal illness is more extraordinary and could not be considered part of ordinary care. However withdrawal of tube feeding is permitted, if it is futile or if the patient is experiencing physical suffering or is in a permanently vegetative state (PVS).[108] Again the Australian Code of Ethical Standards states:

> Continuing to care for a patient is a fundamental way of respecting and remaining in solidarity with that person. When treatments are withheld or withdrawn because they are therapeutically futile or overly-burdensome, other forms of care such as appropriate feeding, hydration and treatment of infection, comfort care and hygiene should be continued. Nutrition and hydration should always be provided to patients unless they cannot be assimilated by a person's body, they do not sustain life, or their only mode of delivery imposes grave burdens on the patient or others.[109]

After death has occurred, the body of the deceased should be tended with care, reverence and in accordance with the religious beliefs and

---

[108] Herzfeld, *Technology and Religion. Remaining human in a co-created world*, 52.
[109] Code of Ethical Standards – 5.12.

desires of the deceased. So we close this chapter with a reflection by Jean Vanier:

> To celebrate death, 'we look it in the face, speak of it, talk about the person who has left us, about their beauty and about our Christian hope, and also about our pain, anguish, anger or even revolt. Death is also celebrated in the way that people pray closely to the dead body, support the bereaved family and live the funeral Eucharist... Just as life can be beautiful, so too can death.[110]

---

[110] Jean Vanier, *Our Journey Home. Rediscovering a common humanity beyond our differences,* translated by Maggie Parham, (Sydney: Hodder and Stoughton, 1997), 136.

# Chapter 9: Pastoral care to the grieving

'Blessed are those who mourn, for they will be comforted' (Mt 5:4). That's the unexpected news: there is a blessing hidden in our grief. Not those who comfort are blessed, but those who mourn! Somehow, in the midst of our tears, a gift is hidden. Somehow, in the midst of our mourning, the first steps of the dance, takes place. Somehow, the cries that well up from our losses belong to our songs of gratitude - **Henri J. M. Nouwen**[111]

Four weeks, three months, ten years later. It doesn't matter how long it's been. Sooner or later, a thousand times over, you're gonna sob - **Alison Sampson**[112]

When my brother's death forced open the door, I stepped into grief and found the compassionate, all-embracing Holy One dwelling within me. I also discovered an inner resiliency I did not know I had, along with an ability to reach beyond self-pity toward a determined hope - **Joyce Rupp**[113]

## Stages of grief

Grief reflects the sadness, sorrow, confusion and possibly guilt that may emerge when people suffer a loss. This loss is of someone or something vital, who or which fills our spirit and heart, brings us alive, and calls forth our energies. It leaves an inner emptiness, and there is disorientation, confusion and anguish. Grief is a process one works

---

[111] Henri J. M. Nouwen, *With Burning Hearts. A Mediation on the Eucharistic Life*, (Maryknoll, New York: Orbis Books, 2002), 28.
[112] Alison Sampson, 'The inevitability of tears,' in *Eureka Street*, 2/11/2010 http://www.eurekastreet.com.au/article.aspx?aeid=23722
[113] Joyce Rupp, *Open the door. A journey to the truth self*, (Notre Dame, Indiana: Sorin Books, 2008), 66-67.

through at their own pace and time, acknowledging loss and the pain of loss. Time to be alone is needed and yet friends can also support one in their grief.

Pastoral care givers are called to be witnesses to each unique pilgrimage of grief and assist grievers to make meaning out of their experiences with death or loss. Colin Murray Parkes in *Bereavement – A Study of Grief in Adult Life*, sets forth five stages of grieving.[114]

1. Alarm/Shock/Numbness – there is always something about the finality of the actual death that is disturbing at a deep level for survivors. Can occur in the first 2 weeks after death or on special occasions. The body needs time to process the changes. Protesting loss occurs through avoidance or denial. Disorientation occurs and sleep disturbance.

2. Searching – time of pining and intense yearning for the dead person, continuing to act as if the person were alive. Can be 4-6 weeks after death but is on and off over the years. They find themself alone and aware that death has occurred. Feelings of anger, powerlessness, anxiety, guilt or helplessness. Recalling their loved one in many ways is necessary.

3. Mitigation – depression and deep despair. The emptiness is painful and difficult. Presence changes to memory. Occurs around the third or fourth month. Friends need to be there at this time to listen and support.

4. Anger/Guilt – emotional turmoil in the fifth and sixth months.

5. Identity/Recovery – About six months later new patterns are formed, new relationships developed and new identity emerge.

---

[114] Colin Murray Parkes, *Bereavement – A Study of Grief in Adult Life*, (UK: Penguin Press, 2010).

Therese Rando produced a model called the 6 R Processes of Mourning.[115] 1. Recognise the loss 2. React to the separation. 3. Recollect and re-experience the deceased and the relationship. 4. Relinquish the old attachments to the deceased 5. Readjust to move adaptively into the new world without forgetting the old 6. Reinvest.[116]

Physical symptoms that grievers may experience include fatigue/exhaustion, disturbed sleep, general aches and pains, headaches, tightness in the throat, heaviness in the chest, empty feeling in the stomach and change in eating habits.

Cognitive symptoms that accompany grieving include nightmares, poor concentration and memory, disorientation and confusion, thoughts are unfocussed and repetitive, decision making is difficult, and preoccupation with death or being alone.

Behavioural symptoms experienced are avoidance of places or activities that are reminders of the event, sighing, social withdrawal and isolation, loss of interest in normal activities, excessive alertness, on the look-out for signs of danger, easily startled, restlessness, significant changes in facial expression and eye contact, confrontational and displaying accident proneness, forgetfulness and regression to immature behaviours, desire to smoke, drink or use drugs, aimlessly wandering, sensing the loved one's presence, hearing their voice, expecting the loved one to come home any minute, assuming mannerisms or traits of the loved one and yearning to be with the loved one, showing significant changes in personal appearance and performance, and becoming less talkative

---

[115] Therese Rando, *Treatment of Complicated Mourning* (Research Press, 1993), 45.
[116] Steven L Jeffers and Harold Ivan Smith, *Finding a sacred oasis in grief. A resource manual for pastoral caregivers,* (Oxford: Radcliffe Publishing, 2007), 91.

Emotional symptoms are fear, numbness and detachment, guilt, irritability, anxiety and panic, need to tell and retell the story of the loved one's death, mood changes, angry at loved one for 'being left', crying at unexpected times, bouts of depression and sadness, unable to respond to praise or reward, lack of enjoyment, and easily tearful.

These symptoms can be distressing, but are part of the natural healing process of adjusting to a very powerful event, making some sense out of what happened, and putting it into perspective. With understanding and support the stress symptoms are usually resolved. A minority of people may develop more serious conditions such as depression, posttraumatic stress disorder, anxiety disorders, or alcohol and drug problems.

## Christian meaning after death

According to Christopher Swift, humans experience meaning as something beyond themselves. That is why the death of a loved one produces such profound grief and loss. With them has departed a certain kind of meaning, a connection with the past and – through their legacy in the world, be it children or art – a contribution to a continuing chain of significance.[117] So in a time of loss and bereavement, when basic questions of life and its meaning are challenged, religious and spiritual influences can be critical.

Theologically, looking at Jesus' teachings, death and resurrection, there are five distinct moments within the paschal cycle, as Ronald Rolheiser suggests:[118]

1. Good Friday – the loss of life, real death
2. Easter Sunday – the reception of new life

---

[117] Swift, *Hospital Chaplaincy in the Twenty-first Century*, 132.
[118] Ronald Rolheiser, *The Holy Longing. The Search for a Christian Spirituality*, (Doubleday, 1999), 147.

3. The Forty days – a time for readjustment to the new and for grieving the old

4. Ascension – letting go of the old and letting it bless you, the refusal to cling

5. Pentecost – the reception of new spirit for the new life that one is already living

Each is part of the process of transformation, of dying and letting go, so as to receive new life and spirit. As a personal, paschal challenge, one might recast the diagram as:[119]

1. Name your deaths

2. Claim your births

3. Grieve what you have lost and adjust to the new reality

4. Do not cling to the old, let it ascend and give you its blessing

5. Accept the spirit of the life that you are in fact living

This cycle is something undergone daily, in every aspect of one's life. Christ spoke of many deaths, of daily deaths, and of many risings and various Pentecosts.

People in all kinds of situations have often shown themselves to be much more resourceful and stronger than expected. They grow to meet disasters and cope with chaos, especially when they are supported and encouraged by family and friends, cultural customs, values and beliefs, societal support organisations such as St Vincent de Paul and religious rituals.

---

[119] Rolheiser, *The Holy Longing. The Search for a Christian Spirituality*, 148.

## Funerals

According to Christopher Swift, very often the experience of death is met largely with silence. Yet the use of ritual acts presents the possibility of meaning in eternal peace, love and happiness, in the face of an otherwise nihilistic experience. Death can become in certain instances a kind of immanent transcendence: a significance for life that emerges out of the grave.[120]

The living presence of God is experienced through the Christian community that cherishes and mourns. As Amy Plantinga Pauw writes, 'The church will gather to celebrate our life and mourn our passing, and confident that the community will care for our family through prayers, visits, and generous hospitality.'[121]

In earlier times Christian funerals involved visitation at home, where the family washed, dressed, sat and waited with the body in recognition that it was still created in the image of God and therefore sacred. The procession then stopped for a service at the Church. The funeral bound the grieving community together and publicly expressed the Church's belief in the gospel, that through the resurrected Jesus we have eternal life with God. In Christian funeral services throughout time, singing hymns, reading Scripture and hearing God's word preached, is how the church displays its hope and belief that life has meaning and significance. The service honours the loved one and allows the bereaved to publicly express that person's significance in their lives and the life of the community. The funeral begins to give shape to grief as the community expresses its faith and ties the swirling emotions following death into the larger story of humanity's redemption. From the Church the gathered would go to the cemetery. In earlier times, the grave was nearby, likely in the churchyard,

---

[120] Swift, *Hospital Chaplaincy in the Twenty-first Century*, 133.
[121] Amy Plantinga Pauw, 'Dying well' in *Living well and dying Faithfully*, John Swinton and Richard Payne (ed), (Grand Rapids, Michigan: William B. Eerdmans Publishing Company, 2009), 20.

so mourners could continue to visit and remember the dead, who, the church believed, remained a part of the church community.[122]

Even though a death of a loved one may have been anticipated for months, the finality of their loss sinks in only after the funeral and burial have taken place. This is the time when a family comes to terms with their relationships with the deceased and start to readjust their lives. A pastoral carer who has been a faithful companion before a death can help families unburden themselves after a death through listening to the reassessment of their decisions and by reaffirming the integrity of their choices.

## Practical care

Grief is selfish, all encompassing, affecting thoughts, emotions, actions, and physical well being. It leaves little energy to attend to self or others.[123] Support is needed, such as a listening presence, enquiring how everything is going, responding understandingly to strong feelings, and encouraging those grieving to express themselves freely.

'I am sorry for your loss' or 'please accept our condolences' are well intentioned remarks but do not really engage the bereaved. Trying to explain away loss in religious or philosophical terms, such as 'Your mother is in a far better place now' are not helpful. A pastoral carer simply shows genuine concern and care with an empathic statement such as, 'It must be very difficult for you.' This allows the bereaved permission to talk about their loss. As Joyce Rupp writes:

> There's nothing wrong with expressing unabashed passion of flailing highly charged outrage about unspeakable suffering upon the divine door and demanding to be heard. No more so than expressing a demure 'please help me' or making a gentle tap of request. When we relate to the

---

[122] Moll, *The Art of Dying* 120.
[123] John Spivey and Shelly Hartwick, 'Grief and Bereavement' in *Hospice, a labor of love*, (St. Louis, Missouri: Chalice Press: 1999), 80.

divine, we do so with our whole being. No part of our self ought to be left out. Pounding is better than pretending things are all right. Trying to beat down the door allows a way to give voice to strong issues. It releases what keeps the soul tethered. However, this pounding cannot go on forever. Nursing bitterness over a loved one's death, perpetually blaming God for a wounded childhood or for the disappointments and struggles of one's life, these indicate that the pounding has to stop. The time comes to desist from beating on the door and begin redirecting one's energy toward eventual reconciliation and acceptance. Whatever the reason for pounding on the door, one hopefully arrives at a place of resolution.[124]

There are various contributions that helpers can make towards proper transition of the grief process such as intervening where appropriate, taking over some things temporarily and passing the responsibility back when they are ready.

Grieving is a form of pilgrimage, a slow process whereby one lets go of a loved one or of life as they move to death. Pastoral pilgrimages are visits to those who are ill or housebound or to the graves of loved ones. This may be among the most meaningful and important pilgrimages one makes.

When there is peri natal loss, other losses also occur. Parents lose their dreams and hopes for the child, lose part of themselves and a part of each other and they lose their future.[125] Mothers who miscarry early in pregnancy may experience the same intensity of grief as those who carry the baby full term resulting in a stillbirth. The appropriate response is to recognise the loss and to validate it. Grieving parents need to be affirmed that their questions and feelings of anger, despair, and frustration are normal and acceptable. The best gift is to listen.[126] Naming, blessing and

---

[124] Rupp, *Open the door. A journey to the truth self*, 53.
[125] Jeffers and Smith, *Finding a sacred oasis in grief. A resource manual for pastoral caregivers*, 41.
[126] Jeffers and Smith, *Finding a sacred oasis in grief. A resource manual for pastoral caregivers*, 45-46.

memorialising, or simply touching and holding the baby are rituals to help say good bye.

In regards to young children, adults must be clear on what they are saying and on what is being heard. If children are told the person who has passed away has gone on a trip, they will expect the person to come back as they do not comprehend the finality of death. Yet when they are told that someone they love has died, they accept that something has happened. Their pain will be in their separation.[127]

A child over the age of six is developmentally tackling the concept of life and death, living and non living things. Children's grief has many dimensions including an apparent lack of feelings, which is more likely to be emotional shock and a protective mechanism. Regression may occur during stressful times where they may wish to be held and rocked or ask a parent to do their shoe lace, because they fear separation from them. Big man syndrome occurs in order to replace the person who is gone and children may begin to express adult behaviour before their time. They may act out, expressing their hurt through anger, resentment and blame. These are explosive emotions behind pain, helplessness, frustration and fear. Loss and loneliness may lead to depression, expressed through lack of interest in themselves, change in appetite or sleeping patterns, nervousness, inability to enjoy life and low self esteem. Eventually reconciliation occurs and children return to stable eating and sleeping patterns and a renewed sense of well being, although grief may stop by briefly during birthdays and holidays.[128]

Unhelpful strategies when caring for adolescents include directives such as 'You will have to be the head of the family now,' being pressured

---

[127] Spivey and Hartwick, *Hospice, a labor of love*, 82-83.
[128] Spivey and Hartwick, *Hospice, a labor of love*, 83-85.

to talk about it; judging them, 'Why are you acting this way?'[129] Accept that you cannot stop the feelings of loss, but you can help the bereaved name and express the pain the loss causes. Grieving people remember most what you choose to be, not what you choose to say.

One simple way to help elders who appear lonely and isolated is for the pastoral carer to visit them at home or call them on the telephone. It reassures them that they are still a part of the community. The elderly may complain of loneliness, health problems, the death of loved ones, changes in their lives etc. It is important to listen to them and validate their feelings. Eventually it may be necessary to gently and patiently encourage them to visit or phone others or overcome their loneliness by helping someone in need.[130]

General practical support in times of grief include surrounding the grieving with love and support, sending letters or cards which express care, regular visits and phone calls. Other practical ways include bringing over a hot meal or doing the grocery shopping, running errands, household repairs, gardening, bringing in the mail and taking out the garbage. Gifts are appreciated such as a bunch of flowers to lighten up the place. Finally prayer, be it for a few moments, over a period of a month, or even over years, help to lift the spirits of those grieving, particularly when they find themselves in a hard place. So let us end with a reflection by Joyce Rupp:

> I sat on the doorstep of my porch, talking on the phone, listening to a newly widowed friend speak of her severe sorrow. In between wrenching tears, she poured out her struggle of attempting to re-engage with a life that no longer included her beloved husband. As I gave full attention to my grieving friend, a young, sleek deer emerged from the woods and stood like a sentinel on the front lawn. At the same time, the

---

[129] http://www.mindmatters.edu.au/verve/_resources/lossgrief.pdf Adapted from Glassock, G. & Rowling L (1992) *Learning to Grieve – Life Skills for Coping with Losses* Newtown, Millennium Books, p105.

[130] Harold G Koenig and Andrew J. Weaver, *Pastoral Care of older adults. Creative pastoral care and counselling,* (Minneapolis: Fortress Press, 1998), 66.

tiny lights of fireflies began twinkling in the night air. I felt caught between two contrasting worlds: the sharp pain in my friend's heart and the alluring beauty of the natural world. Between these two opposites, something unidentified nudged me to pay attention. I let the disparity be there until the phone conversation ended. Then I continued to sit silently on the doorstep, pondering the enticing scene, wondering what stirred inside of me. This movement opened the door to my inner self and led me to look at that part that always wants to be fair. I recognised my strong desire to relieve my friend of her heartache. At that same time, I also trusted she was in a 'growing place' and eventually would be less pained from her loss. From this pause of reflection, I glimpsed divine presence in both areas: a Compassionate Companion embracing hurting ones and a Generous Creator continually revealing abundant splendour. The deer and the fireflies assured me that beauty remains present in the midst of life's turmoil. That evening the door of my heart proved a passageway to gratitude for enduring beauty and a reminder to trust God's strength to be there, especially when the harshness of life shows its face.[131]

---

[131] Joyce Rupp, *Open the door. A journey to the truth self*, 16-17.

# Chapter 10: Sacramental dimension

Are any among you suffering? They should pray. Are any cheerful? They should sing songs of praise. Are any among you sick? They should call for the elders of the church and have them pray over them, anointing them with oil in the name of the Lord. The prayer of faith will save the sick, and the Lord will raise them up; and anyone who has committed sins will be forgiven. Therefore confess your sins to one another, and pray for one another, so that you may be healed. The prayer of the righteous is powerful and effective - **James 5:13-16**

## Our sacramental role

The New Testament is filled with accounts of Jesus' miracles of healing the lame, the blind, the lepers, and even raising the dead. Jesus was a living sacrament of God's compassion to those who suffer. Through Jesus sacramental gestures of healing, people felt the presence and power of God. The disciples also shared Jesus' ministry of healing, as we read in Lk 9:1-6, 'Then Jesus called the twelve together and gave them power and authority over all demons and to cure diseases, and he sent them out to proclaim the kingdom of God and to heal' and again in Mk 6:13, 'They cast out many demons, and anointed with oil many who were sick and cured them.' This pastoral ministry of going to visit those in need and to heal the sick, extends beyond the mission of the twelve disciples, to include all those baptised into Christ who have received the Spirit of love, joy, peace, patience, kindness, generosity, faithfulness, gentleness, and self-control (Gal 5:22-23).

The seven sacraments of baptism, confirmation, Eucharist, reconciliation, marriage, priesthood and anointing of the sick, are symbolic actions in which humans are engaged as believers. Sacraments are expressions by the assembled church, to embody and make accessible the saving work of Christ. They provide a consciousness and living distinguished by freedom, hope and love. Through the sacraments, we participate in the Mystery, which gives meaning and transforms our lives. Church and sacraments are key moments for exploring and articulating one's relatedness, as a divine invitation to life and meaning.

Sacramentals also participate in the paschal character. Sacramentals such as benedictions, blessed objects such as holy water and medals, are symbolic in nature and contribute to sanctifying various occasions in human life, by witnessing to the cosmic dimension of the paschal mystery. In times of suffering and uncertainty Christians turn to religious symbols and acts such as sacraments and sacramentals, that give hope and inspiration to carry on.

## The sacrament of baptism

The sacrament of baptism is about incorporation into the Church, becoming part of a people, being caught up in the divine nature through the bestowal of the Holy Spirit. Baptism allows God's initiative in one's salvation, and offers the gratuitous gift of grace and communitarian care. Paul's letter to the Romans declares, 'But you have received a spirit of adoption. When we cry, 'Abba! Father!' it is that very Spirit bearing witness with our spirit that we are children of God, and if children, then heirs, heirs of God and joint heirs with Christ - if, in fact, we suffer with him so that we may also be glorified with him' (Rom 8:1-17). Baptism is the sign of new life through Christ, uniting the one baptised with Christ and his people. Those baptised are pardoned, cleansed, sanctified and given a new ethical orientation under the Holy Spirit.

Baptism is not only a momentary experience, but a lifelong growth into Christ. The baptised are called to reflect the glory of the Lord as they are continually transformed by the Holy Spirit, 'And all of us... are being transformed into the same image from one degree of glory to another; for this comes from the Lord, the Spirit' (2 Cor 3:18).

As baptised people, we become one in faith, a sacramental people, a dwelling place of God (Eph 4:6), and our role as pastoral care givers to

## Sacrament of the Eucharist

Through celebration of the Eucharist, one witnesses the building up of a community at work. The Holy Spirit, through the Eucharist, gives a foretaste of the Kingdom. 'Those who eat my flesh and drink my blood have eternal life, and I will raise them up on the last day' (Jn 6:54). In the assembled people and the gifts prepared, the hopes, joys and problems of creation, are present, through thanksgiving, memorial and petition.

> The Paschal mystery of Christ . . . participates in the divine eternity, and so transcends all times while being made present in them all. The event of the Cross and Resurrection abides and draws everything toward life.[132]

We are called to translate the mystery of Christian experience into concrete Christian life, to maintain, deepen and perfect the paschal mystery, and to actualise, through worship and sacraments, our Lord's death and resurrection. We must 'walk in newness of life' (Rm 6:4) and 'live by the spirit' (Gal 5:25).

Celebrating the Eucharist liturgy as one who is sick or suffering or as one who comes to serve and heal, or one who comes with grief and sorrow, allows for a deeper gratitude and awe, and increased capacity for suffering, hope and compassion for each person gathered around the table of God.

As Anthony J. Gittins writes, 'The Eucharist of Jesus (the formal institution) took place at table in the Upper Room the night before he died. His actions there are themselves a recapitulation, a concentration or distillation of his entire life. His entire outpouring ministry and

---

[132] *Catechism of the Catholic Church*, 'The Celebration of the Christian Mystery,' (Sydney: St Paul's Publication, 1994), no. 1085.

outpouring death are concrete expressions of feeding, nurturing, healing, restoring, and attending to others' needs - in short, Eucharist that is relatively informal, spontaneous, variegated, and deeply relevant to actual lives and circumstances.'[133] We are called to go forth to feed the hungry, give drink to the thirsty, welcome the stranger, clothe the naked, visit the sick, and come to those in prison (Mt 25:35-36).

The Eucharist is given to us so that Christ's presence may be real in the lives of people, a presence living in our attitudes and values, in our thinking, speaking and the style of life we choose to live. This is the attitude we take from receiving the Eucharist at the altar and entering into relationships at the bedside of an ailing person.

## Sacrament of reconciliation

Like the father of the lost son, God does not stand and wait, but goes forth to seek, as the shepherd sought the lost sheep and as the woman sought the lost coin (Lk 15). God goes in search of sinners. The understanding of the sacrament of reconciliation is that the offer of mercy and forgiveness is available and waiting to be poured out by a loving, compassionate God. As Isaiah reminds us, God is 'waiting to be gracious to you' (Is 30:18).

As Gerard Moore writes, we are drawn to the Sacrament of Reconciliation because of the experience of divine mercy and compassion. In reconciliation, not only are the sins people commit forgiven, but also their sense of estrangement from God, and hostility to the world is healed with acknowledgement and compassion.[134]

As pastoral carers one is called to make people know and experience God's forgiveness and love. The person needs to be reminded that God is willing to forgive them and to overcome their guilt-ridden inability to

---

[133] Anthony J. Gittins, *Called to be sent. Co-Missioned as Disciples Today*, (Missouri: Liguori, 2008), 64-65.

[134] Gerard Moore, *A Hunger for Reconciliation*, (NSW: St Pauls, 2004).

seek forgiveness. To be open to receive this gift means to experience a profound peace.

## Sacrament of anointing of the sick

The rite of anointing of the sick is a sacrament of spiritual and physical healing. The Anointing is offered to the chronically ill, aged and infirm, and those undergoing surgery. The practice of this sacrament includes a pastoral ministry of counsel, prayer, reading the Scriptures, bringing communion and listening to confessions. All those who gather in care around the bed of the ailing are asked to participate in the ceremony as a sign of their concern for those who need their help.

The sacrament of anointing can also be performed as a communal event which usually takes place within a Eucharistic liturgy attended by the ill and carers.

The sacrament is to bring spiritual strength to those who are physically ill. God offers the anointed person grace to overcome anxiety and despair, find comfort, be healed and made whole. The effect is a personal encounter with God, finding meaning in suffering, and hope in death. It is about offering spiritual and physical healing to the sick and also divine forgiveness for those dying.[135]

## Final thought

People experience the life of faith through ritual celebration and experience God through symbols. Therefore, the sacramental symbols and the liturgical rites, provide levels of reality for the person, touching their heart and soul. As we are graced with the Spirit and sent as messengers of Jesus, Christians are invited to be 'Radiating Christ' as Cardinal Newman puts it:

---

[135] Joseph Martos, *Doors to the Sacred: A historical introduction to Sacraments in the Catholic Church*, (Liguori, Missouri: Triumph Books, 1991), 339-340.

Dear Jesus, help me to spread your fragrance everywhere I go. Flood my soul with fragrance everywhere I go. Flood my soul with your spirit and life. Penetrate and possess my whole being so utterly that all my life may only be a radiance of yours. Shine through me, and be so in me that every soul I come in contact with may feel your presence in my soul. Let them look up and see no longer me, but only Jesus! Stay with me, and then I shall begin to shine as you shine so to shine as to be a light to others; the light, O Jesus will be all from you, none of it will be mine, it will be you shining on others through me. Let me thus praise you in the way you love best, by shining on those around me. Let me preach you without preaching, not by words but by my example, by the catching force, the sympathetic influence of what I do; the evident fullness of the love my heart bears for you. Amen.[136]

---

[136] 'Radiating Christ' by Cardinal Newman
http://lordcalls.com/dailyprayer/radiating-christ-prayer-by-cardinal-newman

# Chapter 11: The stations of the Cross – Accompanying the sick and dying

This final chapter offers an adapted Stations of the Cross that expresses the anguish and suffering that Jesus experienced and continues to be experienced by many who are suffering. It may be prayed alone or with others, to strengthen one's faith as they journey on.

### The First Station: Jesus is condemned to death

Pilate sentences Jesus to death. It is the final decision which will not be overturned. Much like a death sentence passed over us when the prognosis from a doctor is not good. It is like a dark shadow engulfs us. And as the doctor turns away, we turn to God. It is all unexpected, unjust and we scream, 'Why me?' Can nothing be done? But just as Pilate washes his hands clean, God directs us to look ahead. There is another path to tread . . .

### The Second Station: Jesus carries his Cross

So the treatments begin. Chemotherapy, bitter pills, long stays in hospitals . . . but like the Cross, they only weaken and burden. Sickness entails pain, medical treatment, lengthy waits. One has no choice but to carry the Cross, to swallow the medicine, to be bedridden . . .

### The Third Station: Jesus falls the first time

We stumble and fall as we learn to walk with crutches, to endure the excruciating pain each time we rise, to get up after a sleepless night . . . Things, simple things, become chores, harder to do, but needing to be done . . . we slowly begin to feel like we are less than all there, not fully here, not completely present.

### The Fourth Station: Jesus meets his mother

There are those who always care, who know how, know what we want without asking and offer that gentle touch. We may be the victim and they may be ever patient, but look closely and our anguish is theirs. Are they too not the victim? Sometimes there are simply no words to exchange, but mere presence is enough. A touch . . . a gentle smile . . . a wipe of a tear, but whose tear?

### The Fifth Station: Jesus falls a second time

Things do not get easier in this journey with pain. Should we get up? What for? Does trying really achieve anything, let alone hoping? But there is still something left in this old tank for now. The pain won't get the better of us. We can go on. Not because we want this pain, but because we want to be stronger than it. Our time is not yet up. Our friends still visit our bedside.

### The Sixth Station: Veronica wipes the face of Jesus

Nurses and doctors know how and what to do. Family, kin and friends are good to have around also, just to do what is so basic and yet needed. We cannot live alone. We truly need at least one other by our bedside. Washing and wiping, cleaning and trimming, it is so good physically and mentally. Care is good for the soul.

### The Seventh Station: Jesus meets the women of Jerusalem

It's important to be there when the time beckons. To be in solidarity with those who suffer. But it is more important to come with good intentions, a discerning heart, a touch of warmth and compassion. We may not achieve any miracles together, but at least we would have enriched one another's lives.

### The Eighth Station: Jesus falls a third time

We know we cause others and ourselves great anguish, harm and suffering. However there is no overcoming it. We just have to get up and go on, knowing we will fall again. The journey may be ending but we still want to walk with dignity. Give us reason to keep going.

### The Ninth Station: Simon carries Jesus' Cross

One's burden is also another's. The bell tolls for you and I. Parents who carry their children's pain, a spouse who tends to their partner's needs, or a sibling who shares the burden of their brother or sister. It may be just a while, or months, or even years. Does it make them stronger or does it break them? In sickness and in health so the vows go.

### The Tenth Station: Jesus is stripped of his garments

In those final days, all dignity is gone. All independence just a mere nostalgia. All dreams dissipate. Only a cold, harsh reality remains, naked and exposed. Yet despite all that was meant to be important in life disappearing, we still are. Deep within us runs life's course, what truly matters. What will we do with this running river of life?

### The Eleventh Station: Jesus is nailed to the Cross

Others suffer too, next door to us. We are not alone and yet this final journey is a personal one. Pain, anguish and suffering mark it. Perhaps it is best to end it here and now. But remember us not as we are now, but what we were in better days.

### The Twelfth Station: Jesus dies

So we all die. We close our eyes. It is time to release our spirit. Time to let go, hoping we have made some sort of positive contribution to the lives of others and to the world at large. Farewell, we will miss you all as we take our leave.

**The Thirteenth Station: Jesus is taken down from the Cross**

Grief sets in. Our loved ones are enfolded in caring arms. Tears shed once more, as the body is washed one last time. The viewing floods the mind with past memories. The torment, pain and suffering has had its final days. The body is now laid to rest.

**The Fourteenth Station: Jesus is buried**

Life goes on and on. Taken down and buried. Sealed but not forgotten. We feel their presence, miss their character, and yet every once in a while we catch glimpses of them in their children and grandchildren, in an aunt or nephew. Life holds many wonders and offers them to us in a resurrected form.

# Bibliography

Arandra S, Buchanan J, Green G, Hodder P. 'The practice of palliative care. In *The creative option of palliative care.* Hodder P, Turley A., eds. (Melbourne: City Mission, 1989), 11-33.

Anderson, Ray S. *Spiritual Caregiving as Secular Sacrament. A Practical Theology for Professional Caregivers.* London: Jessica Kingsley Publishers, 2003: 163-178

Australian Bureau of Statistics
http://www.agedcare.org.au/PUBLICATIONS-&-RESOURCES/General-pdfs-images/ACSA%20Fact%20Sheet%201%202008-%20An%20Ageing%20Australia.pdf

Akhurst, Kim., Story producer. Story researcher: Jeannine Baker. 'Work, Later On' *Compass programme*, 19 September 2010.

Therese J. Borchard, 'Let Me Live Until I Die: An Interview with Thea Bowman.' Accessed 3rd March 2012.
http://psychcentral.com/blog/archives/2010/10/17/let-me-live-until-i-die-an-interview-with-thea-bowman/

Calhoun, Gerald J. *Pastoral Companionship. Ministry with seriously-ill persons and their families.* New York: Paulist Press, 1986.

Carey, Lindsay B., Christopher J. Newell and Bruce Rumbold, 'Pain Control and Chaplaincy in Australia' in *Journal of Pain and Symptom Management* 32, no. 6, December 2006:589-601.

*Catechism of the Catholic Church*, 'The Celebration of the Christian Mystery,' (Sydney: St Paul's Publication, 1994),

Catholic Health Australia http://www.cha.org.au/site.php?id=24

Chittister, Joan D. *Scarred by Struggle, Transformed by Hope.* Grant Rapids, Michigan: William B Eerdmans Pub. Co., 2003.

Chittister, Joan D. *Welcome to the wisdom of the world.* Grand Rapids, Michigan: William B. Eerdmans, 2007.

Code of ethics for Catholic Social Services Australia 2006, 1.2. http://catholicsocialservices.org.au/system/files/Code_of_Ethics_06.pdf

Code of Ethical Standards – Catholic Health Australia for Catholic Health and Aged Care Services in Australia. http://www.stvincents.com.au/assets/files/pdf/CodeofEthicalStandards.pdf

Covey, Stephen R. *The 7 habits of highly effective people.* 2004.

Culpepper, R. Alan. *The New Interpreters Bible: Luke* Vol IX, Nashville: Abingdon, 1995.

Dunman, Maxie. *The workbook on Coping as Christians.* Nashville, Tennessee, The Upper Room, 1993.

Eckersley, Richard. 'Values and visions: youth and the failure of modern Western Culture' in *Youth Studies* Vol. 14, No. 1, Autumn 1995.

Evans, Abigail Rian. 'Healing in the Midst of Dying: A Collaborative Approach to End-of-Life Care' in *Living well and dying Faithfully,* John Swinton and Richard Payne (ed), Grand Rapids, Michigan: William B. Eerdmans Publishing Company, 2009:165-187.

Frankl, Viktor E. *Man's search for Meaning.* Boston: Beacon Press, 2006.

Gittins, Anthony J. *Called to be sent. Co-Missioned as Disciples Today.* Missouri: Liguori, 2008.

Gittins, Anthony J. *Reading the Clouds. Mission Spirituality for New Times.* Strathfield: St Pauls, 1999.

Glavan, Denise. 'Death and dying' in *Hospice, a labor of love.* St. Louis, Missouri, 1999: 5-13.

Gollnick, James. *Religion and Spirituality in the Life Cycle,* NY: Peter Lang, 2008.

Graham, Elaine L. *Words made flesh. Writings in pastoral and practical Theology.* London: SCM Press, 2009;135-152.

Groome, Thomas H. *What makes us Catholic. Eight gifts for life.* NY: HarperSanFrancisco, 2002.

Habel, Norman C. 'In defence of God the Sage' in *The Voice from the whirlwind: Interpreting the Book of Job* by Leo G Perdue and W. Clark Gilpin editors. Nashville: Abingdon Press, 1992.

Herzfeld, Noreen. *Technology and Religion. Remaining human in a co-created world.* West Conshohocken, PA: Templeton Press, 2009.

Hughes, Gerard W. *Oh God Why? A spiritual journey towards meaning, wisdom and strength.* Oxford: The Bible Reading Fellowship, 1996.

Jeffers, Steven L. and Harold Ivan Smith, *Finding a sacred oasis in grief. A resource manual for pastoral caregivers,* Oxford: Radcliffe Publishing, 2007.

Julian of Norwich. *Revelations of Divine Love.* London: Penguin Books, 1998.

Kimble, Melvin A. 'Pastoral Care of the Elderly' in *The Journal of Pastoral Care.* Vol XLI, No. 3, September 1987:270-279.

Koenig, Harold G and Andrew J. Weaver. *Pastoral Care of older adults. Creative pastoral care and counselling.* Minneapolis: Fortress press, 1998: 21-23, 65-69, 83-91.

Lawrence, Robert M., Julia Head, Georgina Christodoulou, Biljana Andonovska, Samina Karamat, Anita Duggal, Jonathan Hillam and Sarah Eagger. 'Spiritual advisors and old age psychiatry in the United Kingdom' in *Mental health, Religion and Culture* 11 (3), 2008:273-286.

Leonard, Richard SJ, *Where the Hell is God?* New Jersey: HiddenSpring, 2010.

Lopez, Frank. *Applied Pastoral Care: A Contextual Approach*, Hunters Hill: Marist Centre for Pastoral Care, 1995.

Martos, Joseph. *Doors to the Sacred: A historical introduction to Sacraments in the Catholic Church.* Liguori, Missouri: Triumph Books, 1991.

Mason, Michael; Andrew Singleton and Ruth Webber. *The Spirit of Generation Y. Young People's spirituality in a changing Australia.* Victoria: John Garret Publishing, 2007.

McGilvray, Jill. *God's love in action. Pastoral Care for everyone.* Victoria: Acorn Press, 2009.

Moll, Rob. *The Art of Dying.* Downers Grove, Illinois: IVP Books, 2010.

Moore, Gerard. *A Hunger for Reconciliation.* NSW: St Pauls, 2004.

Mudie, Ian. 'My Father Began as a God.' Accessed 3rd March 2012. http://www.lakemac.infohunt.nsw.gov.au/library/links_level.asp?Level=2 &LevelID=151

Notaro, Carlo. *Comedy, Tragedy and Religion*. New York, State University of New York Press, 1999.

Notaro, Carlo. 'Ministering to the dying: Passage through fear, guilt and grief.' In *Camillianum* 6(1995): 251-267.

Notaro, Carlo. 'Experience and Concepts of Health.' In *Camillianum Magazine: International Magazine for Pastoral Theology of Healthcare*, 1991, 89-92.

Nouwen, Henri J. M. *With Burning Hearts. A Mediation on the Eucharistic Life*. Maryknoll, New York: Orbis Books, 2002.

Nouwen, Henri J. M. *Reaching Out. The three movements of the Spiritual Life*. New York: Image Books Double day, 1986.

Oriah. 'Mountain Dreaming.' In *The Invitation*. San Francisco: HarperONE, 1999.

Parkes, Colin Murray. *Bereavement – A Study of Grief in Adult Life*. UK: Penguin Press, 2010.

Pattison, Stephen. *The challenge of Practical Theology. Selected Essays*. London: Jessica Kingsley Publishers, 2007: 132-143.

Pauw, Amy Plantinga. 'Dying well' in *Living well and dying Faithfully*, John Swinton and Richard Payne (ed), Grand Rapids, Michigan: William B. Eerdmans Publishing Company, 2009:17-29.

Pope John Paul II. Letter to the Elderly, 1999. http://www.vatican.va/holy_father/john_paul_ii/letters/documents/hf_jp-ii_let_01101999_elderly_en.html

Pope John Paul II. Apostolic Letter *Salvifici doloris* 11th Feb 1984. http://www.vatican.va/holy_father/john_paul_ii/apost_letters/documents/hf_jp-ii_apl_11021984_salvifici-doloris_en.html

Pope John Paul II. *On the Christian Meaning of Human Suffering.* Boston: Pauline Books and Media, 1984.

Rahner, Karl. 'God of my Sisters and Brothers,' in *Karl Rahner. Spiritual Writings.* Edited by Philip Endean. Maryknoll: Orbis Books, 2004: 107-111.

Rahner, Karl. *Theological Investigations.* Herder and Herder, Vol. VII.

Rando, Therese. *Treatment of Complicated Mourning.* Research Press, 1993.

Robinson, Geoffrey. *Travels in Sacred Places,* Blackburn, Victoria: Harper Collins Religious, 1997.

Rolheiser, Ronald. *The Holy Longing. The Search for a Christian Spirituality.* Doubleday, 1999.

Rupp, Joyce. *Open the door. A journey to the truth self.* Notre Dame, Indiana: Sorin Books, 2008.

Sampson, Alison. 'The inevitability of tears,' in *Eureka Street,* 2/11/2010. http://www.eurekastreet.com.au/article.aspx?aeid=23722

Sayers, Dorothy L. *Christian Letters to a Post-Christian World.* Grand Rapids, Michigan: William B. Eeermans Publishing Company, 1969.

Spivey, John and Shelly Hartwick. 'Grief and Bereavement' in *Hospice, a labor of love.* St. Louis, Missouri: Chalice Press: 1999, 73-85.

Stoddard, Sandol. *The Hospice Movement.* New York: Vintage Books, 1992.

Swift, Christopher. *Hospital Chaplaincy in the Twenty-first Century*, England: Ashgate, 2009.

Townsend, Loren. *Introduction to Pastoral Counselling*. Nashville: Abingdon Press, 2009.

Tristram H. Jr. 'Generic chaplaincy: providing spiritual care in a post-Christian age' in *Christian Bioethics* 4, no.3, 1998.

Vanier, Jean. *Our Journey Home. Rediscovering a common humanity beyond our differences*. Translated by Maggie Parham. Sydney: Hodder and Stoughton, 1997.

Vanier, Jean. *A Door of Hope*. Translated by Teresa de Bertodano. London: Hodder and Stoughton, 1996.

Vardey, Lucinda, Editor. *Mother Teresa. A Simple path*. Sydney: Rider, 1995.

Walker, Esther Mary. *Beatitudes for Friends of the Aged*, Year unknown. http://www.theexaminer.org/volume7/number2/aged.htm

Wiesel, Elie. *Night*. London: Penguin Books, 2006.

www.ingramcontent.com/pod-product-compliance
Lightning Source LLC
LaVergne TN
LVHW051745080426
835511LV00018B/3238